# Humorous
# Hassle

## 101 TRUE TRAVEL AND LIFE STORIES TO MAKE YOU LAUGH AND SMILE

WHERE IS THE FOG?

BLAST! I'VE JUST MISSED MEETING THE ALIENS

A DIFFERENT KIND OF POLITICAL CLEAN SWEEP

## ANDREW P. WILTSHIRE

PROFITS FROM EVERY SALE WILL BE DONATED TO CHARITY

**All profits from the sale of this book will be donated to
The Salvation Army Homelessness Services Charity**

The Salvation Army is a registered Charity in England (214779) Wales (214779),
Scotland (SC009359) and the Republic of Ireland (CHY6399)

Further copies of this book can be purchased from the publisher:
The Arthington Publishing Company Ltd
One Ivy House, Hopkirk Close, Danbury, Chelmsford, Essex CM3 4PP England

Please telephone: (+44) (0)7831 774499 or email: info@tap.uk.com
or visit the website: www.tap.uk.com and complete the purchase page

**Further information about a fund raising talk,
with photographs, based on this book,
can also be found on the website: www.tap.uk.com**

Printed and bound by: Blackwell Print Ltd, Great Yarmouth, NR30 3LA

A catalogue record for this book is available from the British Library.
Paperback ISBN number: 978-0-9934090-2-8

This book is dedicated to Noah, Zachary and Harry
'Future travellers in this exciting world'

# CONTENTS

## PREFACE

It was in the mid-1990s, whilst returning from a trip to the US after an assignment with a civil aviation division of Britain's largest aerospace organisation, that I realised my experience – of being on an American Airlines 747 as it ran out of fuel approaching the Welsh coast – was one worth remembering!

Above all, this was because a colleague, who had had the foresight to be on a different plane, and other listeners since, did not believe my description of the nonchalant way the pilot announced we did not need to help him buy more fuel when (if) we landed. He said it would be OK; he was carrying the company credit card.

I experienced similar reactions of disbelief whilst also telling the true stories of being hijacked when travelling from Beijing in China, having my ears set on fire in Istanbul and finding, disappointingly, that there was no fog on London's Orbital Motorway, the M25. This was at several dinners in the Institute of Directors' headquarters in Pall Mall, London, and I began to wonder if it was only to me that such events happened.

Being in the fortunate position, or not, depending on your keenness on taking flights from Heathrow, of travelling the world during my management consulting career, I enjoyed (?) waiting for ferries, planes, taxis and trains. At such 'quality times' I realised I ought to be noting the challenges I was experiencing – if only to see if I could learn from them and try to avoid them on future projects.

Accordingly, I began to write about them in a series of pocket notebooks. I hope you don't think that's sad; perhaps you do the same? If you don't, and are often travelling, then I urge you to begin the same habit so that you, too, have something to look back on as your past becomes a blur.

Because of my approach, I am now the proud owner of very many memories triggered by these reminders, several of which are included in this compilation. I learnt as time went by that not only did I have a great number of testing experiences I could recount but also, from the amused reactions I was getting when I did, others shared my belief that a laugh and a smile helps to alleviate the hassle of such situations, as well as underpin the hope that they will be successfully overcome or resolved. They then wanted to tell me their own stories!

(As an example of those who have also had interesting experiences, and now look back with relief, make sure you read the story about the innocent campers in the African bush not being eaten by lions!)

I, therefore, used my extensive Outlook address book to invite people

I knew to refer to their notebooks or, more likely, just recall stressful life or travel situations, which they would be happy to share in creating a publication that, when sold, would raise funds for a worthy charity. The Salvation Army is one that puts such monies directly to the point of need, across a range of activities providing care, support and services in the whole community. This is without discrimination or funds going towards excessive administration or executive salaries. The stories you are about to read are the result of the replies I received.

However, before you begin reading them, I must apologise to those who have helped me develop my manuscript over, what is now, several years. This won't be the first book that has experienced various development delays from conception to publication. Notwithstanding these, sometimes very frustrating situations, I was motivated to continue by recalling the following comment of Ms Beth Tweddle, Gymnastic bronze medallist at the London 2012 Olympics. When asked what kept her going – to win, eventually, at the 'ripe old age' (for the sport) of 27 – she replied, 'With hard work there is always a way to succeed to achieve your hopes and dreams.' Publishing this book is one of mine. Whether you are a contributor, or a supporter, when you now look at the finished work, I trust you feel it's been worth the wait and that, in bringing it to life, the sales achieved will help meet our fund raising ambitions.

## *APPRECIATION*

I am especially grateful to the many friends, international business clients, published authors, journalists from national newspapers and public figures from the worlds of politics and entertainment who have helped me by providing their anecdotes. Each of them has donated their time to do this in writing or by phoning me. It has been a pleasure to correspond with everyone, as well as discuss your various reminiscences. Some were long, some short; some of you sent several, some just one. Whatever type, they were each appreciated. I hope you feel I have not edited the spirit out of them. All were provided with the purpose of making readers laugh and smile as they learn how these contributors faced and overcame true life and travel situations – but who, perhaps, did not relax until they were safely back home!

You will find their names and contribution/s acknowledged, and then indexed, at the back of the book.

## *INTRODUCTION*

As each of the people I contacted tentatively accepted my invitation, I urged them to see that their stories need not only be humorous travel ones but also about real-life situations or family reminiscences. To set the scene for what I had in mind, I sent them the 'How nice to meet you. What do you do?' (chapter 1) and 'Have you tried our flying beer?' (chapter 3) stories and the replies I received certainly built on those two examples.

I am delighted to take proud ownership of the item that immediately follows this introduction. It's the story of the unexpected experience that started me thinking about creating this book. I hope you find it as amusing as I did (once I had calmed down afterwards) and that you also enjoy my story about almost meeting aliens in their spaceships in chapter 1.

There is an additional reason for going to print. That is a desire to provide you, the reader, with something humorous that helps you take your mind off whatever demands you are facing. If the following stories do that, then the purpose of my mission, and that of all those involved with it, will have been achieved.

For, in recent times, there has been a rash of scientific evidence extolling the therapeutic value of laughter. This evidence suggests that forgetting, for a short while, a challenging situation, perhaps by reading something that makes us laugh and smile opens up neural pathways. Chuckling can help our nervous systems beat stress, stave off tiredness, and produce positive and effective thinking.

'Getting away from it all', say on a holiday, is also a way of achieving these reactions. However, it is known that the thrilling disorientation of arriving in a foreign land and grappling with its mysteries and complexities seems to unlock hidden dimensions of creativity! Apparently, this happens as our brains re-wire in an attempt to acclimatise and cope with different surroundings. Additionally, and as a knock-on benefit, we often find that when we return home, we are able to solve – or at least cope better with – the problems in our lives that originally seemed insurmountable.

I suggest that's not only to do with experiencing something new but it's also having the ability to remember a different or thought-provoking experience positively. This may be because some aspect of it makes you laugh and smile about it 'once the dust has settled'.

Unfortunately, Victor Meldrew, the British television character, who became increasingly frustrated by being embroiled in complex misunderstandings, or the victim of bureaucracy, did not often laugh like this. Rather, we laughed at him during situations seen in a long-running BBC TV comedy show of the 1990s, especially, when he used the phrase that is now the title of chapter 1 ('I don't believe it!).

Of course you could, and perhaps always did (even still do), blame someone else, like many of those involved in the stories in chapter 2 ('Was it something that was said?') may have done.

Similarly, as you read about the strange habits, foods and excessive alcohol experiences in chapter 3 ('Was it something that was eaten or drunk?'), you may remember your own comparable trials, when you also blamed someone else for your accident, hangover or tummy ache.

Terry Wogan, the Radio and TV celebrity, was famous for posing the question I have used as the title of chapter 4 ('Is it me, or is it them?'). Perhaps you too can admit to asking, or thinking, that same question as the anecdotes in the chapter trigger your memories.

Those who actually experienced and wrote about their trials and tribulations in chapter 5 ('Getting there and, hopefully, getting back') and chapter 6 ('Travel – it really does broaden the mind') may well have been unhappy at the time of the events. Indeed, those caught up in the anecdotes described in the latter chapter might not agree with the sentiment implied by its title at all. However, the act of having to cope with a problem of translation, a confusing transport timetable or an alarming/dangerous situation certainly forced them to think in new, unexpected and possibly beneficial ways.

Lastly, as the management consulting saying goes, 'When you're up to your neck in alligators, it is difficult to remind yourself that your initial objective was to drain the swamp.' I suggest examples in chapter 7 ('Life is stranger than fiction') reinforce that truism.

Postscript: I am sure the cartoons by Andrew Marsh will encourage further smiles whilst you are reading as he illustrates the challenge that the English language often provides to those who use it easily and those who do not.

## *INVITATION*

To strengthen the enjoyment theme I mentioned earlier, I also asked the contributors to allow me to create a punch line for each story. If these, or indeed any of the stories, inspire you to say, 'I can beat that,' well then – please get writing and send me your story in about 400 words. Write to me at info@tap.uk.com.

Whatever your reaction, I trust that the travel stories don't put you off visiting any of the places that we might have identified, but rather prompt you to record what happens if you do. Who knows? Your experiences, and yet more from my own 'library', might make it to a second edition and raise even more funds for charity.

**Thank you for buying the book. I look forward to you enjoying it. APW, Danbury, Essex, 2015**

Postscript: I have learned from many international scenarios that the only three statements you need to be able to say – in the language of the country you are visiting or working in – are 'Yes', 'No' and 'My friend pays'.

More profoundly, and seriously, I invite you to consider the words of Clifton Fadiman (American intellectual, author and television personality):

'When you travel, remember that a foreign country is not designed to make you comfortable. It is designed to make its own people comfortable.'

**You may wish to recall these sentiments when you are next travelling abroad.**

## *WHERE IS THE FOG?*

### *(The story that inspired this book)*

As part of a major long-term World Bank development project, I was privileged to be chosen to lead the hosting of the first month-long delegation of 30 Chinese government officials visiting the UK from Tianjin, the third city of the People's Republic of China. This group included Mr Lin, the fourth Mayor, responsible for the 27 industries in a city of 10 million inhabitants, so it was a visit of great political importance and sensitivity.

After six months of careful planning, including the development of a series of study tours, lectures and visits to major British industrial organisations, I thought I was ready for anything. I had been briefed by members of the British Civil Service and the staff of the Chinese Embassy in London, hired the services of two Mandarin speaking interpreters and a 40-seat executive coach, so what could possibly go wrong?

I had also arranged to collect the officials from Terminal 3 at Heathrow, having been given permission to have my coach parked directly at the exit of the airport building. Upon the arrival of the delegation, everything proceeded smoothly, with Passport Control quickly checking their visas and the airport staff collecting and loading the groups' many suitcases into the coach. I felt good and in control, especially with a police motorbike escort leading us from the airport, onto the approach road system joining the M25 orbital motorway around London, and towards our four-star hotel about 30 minutes away.

Imagine my horror when the delegation's interpreter came to the front of the coach and demanded, 'You must stop the coach!' I replied that this was impossible as it was against the law and we would certainly be in trouble with the policeman, who was driving in front of the coach, with his motorbike's rear light flashing brightly.

The interpreter stressed that this was a personal order from the Mayor and, therefore, must be obeyed! Accordingly, I asked the coach driver to steer us onto the hard shoulder of the motorway and, once stationary, I walked to the rear of the coach where the Mayor sat.

With much politeness, he asked me, in Mandarin, which in turn was translated into English, 'Where is the Fog?'

It was only just early autumn so I did not know what he meant. We were not expecting that sort of weather. From out of the corner of my eye, I could see the police officer parking his motorbike and walking back towards us talking into his walkie-talkie.

By now, there was much discussion between the Mayor and his interpreter, who then gave me the following explanation:

This was the first time that the delegation members had left China and they had been led to believe that England, especially in the London area, was always clouded in heavy fog. The official interpreter continued to explain that many of them had been prepared for the visit by watching British films authorised by the Chinese government, such as the famous 1946 David Lean production of Charles Dickens's 'Great Expectations'. This was a story set in the conditions they expected to see from the motorway!

As I returned to the front, the officer boarded the coach and, with a very serious look, asked me, luckily, quietly, 'What the **** do you think you're doing, stopping on the motorway?' I could only make the false reply that the Mayor, who he knew was the most important person present, needed the toilet, but I had asked him to wait as we would soon be at the hotel so, we had better get going quickly!

Fortunately, two weeks later, the weather produced the very type of conditions the Mayor had expected. I would like to believe the delegates thought I had arranged it just for them as Mr Lin, who by then, I had learnt, could read and speak English very well …

*… had privately told me how much he was enjoying the morning fog (actually autumn mist) that had now arrived!*

## 1)   I DON'T BELIEVE IT!

You may recall that this quotation was made famous by Victor Meldrew, the fictional character played by Richard Wilson in the popular BBC One sitcom, 'One Foot in the Grave'. The archetypal grumpy old man, Meldrew, is a foil for the bothersome aspects of children, cars, animals, power cuts and next-door neighbours. Perhaps you remember watching the TV show?

Not wishing to over-emphasise the 'grumpiness aspect', I nevertheless suggest that you have at some point in your life, and whatever your age, found yourself pondering a situation that has perplexed or frustrated you, especially when you felt your experience was the result of somebody else's actions. You believed you were the innocent party!

However, looking back, you realise that you were subconsciously using the same phrase, whether you knew Victor or not, as the statement encapsulates the human reaction of stupefaction or bafflement.

Mind you, on a few occasions (?) you may also have used stronger language than this chapter's heading – perhaps like the victim in the story 'Stop thief! That's my case!', which follows, did.

*Newspaper headings and notices to start your reading …*

GROWING RESPECT
Police in the Indian state of Madhya Pradesh are being paid 30 rupees (36p) a month extra to grow moustaches because commanders believe it will help them command more respect.
*This book's author is impressed – he has one too! (But he is not sure it works for him in the same way as the Indian police intended.)*

SCIENCE EXPERT SAYS COLD WAVE LINKED TO TEMPERATURES
*Who would have thought it – how much does he earn?*

MAN KILLS HIMSELF BEFORE SHOOTING WIFE AND DAUGHTER
*I think even Sherlock Holmes would have been baffled by this case.*

Seen on the card that came with a digital tyre gauge:
When measuring more than one tyre please turn off the unit in-between each measurement so allowing the unit to re-collaborate …
*Who with? The other tyres or the gauges sent over from China?*

New York hotel's rules and regulations:
GUESTS ARE REQUESTED NOT TO SMOKE OR DO OTHER DISGUSTING BEHAVIOURS IN BED
*(Spoilsports!)*

*Text on a poster erected by the English Heritage organisation at the site of the Battle of Hastings, The Abbey, High St, Battle, Hastings, East Sussex during the bad weather of October 2014:* THE BATTLEFIELD IS CLOSED DUE TO ADVERSE WEATHER CONDITIONS.

*In 1066 it was even more waterlogged. Today, our Health and Safety culture deems it too dangerous for tourists because it is wet. Perhaps the thousands of Norman and English soldiers who met a bloody end there wished they'd seen a similar notice before they started fighting.*

PRIVATE BUSINESS
It was a noticeable feature of the design of the old lavatories inside the Stalinist-influenced Beijing Central Railway station that neither the men's nor women's cubicles had full-sized doors. The small modesty panels that were provided, on weak hinges, meant these 'privies' were far from private. This was especially the case when you realised that the booths were positioned exactly opposite each other – so there was no chance of any concealment of your business therein. (You might be doing something against the state?)

## BLAST! I'VE JUST MISSED MEETING THE ALIENS

On Thursday, 5 August 2011, the Daily Telegraph newspaper published a full-page article about the recent release of secret files held by the United Kingdom Government in the 1950s. These contained reports doubting the existence of Unidentified Flying Objects (UFOs), spaceships and aliens. Recalling a personal link to the evidence that they did, I wrote to the Editor on Saturday, 7 August, as follows:

'Aliens have regularly visited us for some time. In my hotel room in Tianjin in November 1993, I found they had left a copy of their 'Guide to Aliens visiting China'. Article 3 required them to present a valid passport and travel permit. As the room was empty, I assumed they had done so, and moved on, leaving the booklet for the next arrival.'

This letter, reproduced here with permission, was published on page 19 of the Tuesday, 10 August 2011 edition. My fifteen minutes of fame at last.

**Returning often to China, and this hotel, I kept the booklet with me just in case some of these 'visitors' reappeared and wanted to read it!**

## HONOUR THY NEIGHBOUR – PLEASE

When my husband and I got married we bought and moved into the house next door to my husband's family home, thus making my father-in-law (and remaining children at home) my next door neighbour. I knew that he was slightly eccentric and that he was always inexplicably short of money, despite running a thriving family electrical business and associated shop.

One evening, I came home from work to find some bricks had been removed from the side wall of our house, making a hole big enough for him to connect his house up to our electrical supply, so that we were being billed for all the electricity he was using next door.

Another time, I returned to find that he had wired his garden shed up to our telephone connection, and inserted posts into our lawn carrying the cable across our garden into his shed. Whenever he wanted to make a phone call, he would retire to his shed and call at our expense.

The odd thing was that none of his (ten) children seemed to find anything odd about his behaviour, and accepted it as if it were perfectly normal, so it seemed I was the only one feeling annoyed by his behaviour. This made me wonder …

### … if he (or they) knew the eighth commandment?

Postscript: In case you have forgotten this one – it's in verse 15 of chapter 20 in the book of Exodus. 'Thou shalt not steal.'

## HOW NICE TO MEET YOU. WHAT DO YOU DO?

I decided to take a three-day bus journey from Phoenix to Miami. As I boarded the bus, my mother's last words were ringing in my ears. 'Oh darling, do be careful.'

I made my way to the only place left. It was on the back window row. Unfortunately, due to the enormous size of the passenger already in situ, I only had half a seat left to sit on. He was a big African American, with earphones and a rather grumpy manner! Everything was fine whilst he sat still, but every now and then he would adjust his headphones and as he did, there was the most powerful smell of body odour.

Little did I know this was going to be the least of my worries.

After being on the road for a while, the passenger in front of me decided to turn around and chat. He was a skinny, unshaven, old man with white, wild hair sticking out of a rather thick woolly hat. Considering it was 40°C outside, I thought this was certainly rather odd.

At first, he seemed normal but, with the conversation turning to his wife, he then said, without a hint of irony:

'Hell, my wife was a bad woman – she was so bad I killed her. It's OK, no one knows about it 'cos I chopped her up and put her in the freezer.'

Well, I did as all good English girls should.

**I said politely, 'Oh, how interesting, tell me more.'**

## I'D BE EMBARRASSED IF THIS HAPPENED ON THE LONDON UNDERGROUND

At the beginning of 2000, I was presenting a marketing planning and strategy workshop in the centre of Beijing. Travelling each day between my hotel and the conference venue, I'd soon noticed how crowded the underground station platforms were. (We think we've got overcrowding in London.)

With my Chinese host pushing our way into an evening train home, it was clear we would both have to stand as all the seats were taken. In fact, we didn't need to stand, just lean against all the other passengers who were crowded into the carriage.

Imagine then, my embarrassment when my host, without any explanation or invitation, took the arms of a young man sitting directly in front of me and pulled him straight up and out of his seat. I was then instructed to sit down quickly. Being older than the onlookers, I was hoping they were thinking I needed the rest more than they did.

Unlike the London Underground, they didn't have the little symbol on the window that said, 'Please give up this seat to an elderly person.'

**If this was a passenger's typical action, perhaps they didn't need to!**

Postscript: Readers should also enjoy the chapter 3 story, 'Embarrassed by a "Big Mac" in Beijing'. It involves the same cultural characteristic as this underground experience.

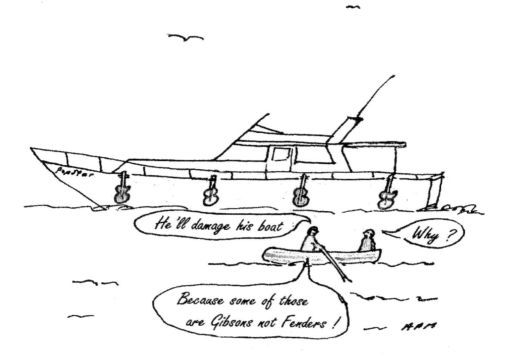

## I WAS GLAD THEY WEREN'T OPERATING ON ME

Besides, as mentioned in the first story, hosting Chinese government officials in the UK (and explaining why we did not have the fog they were expecting), I also had to spend many months in Tianjin on mainland China. Part of my brief, whilst there, was to conduct business research, other times to present lectures to a wide variety of delegates in offices and factories across the city.

At these events it was particularly important to illustrate various concepts using acetate overhead projector slides, created in Mandarin, accompanied by explanations presented through my interpreter. (This was in a time before PowerPoint and laptops!)

Electricity to power the office lighting and projector bulb was therefore essential, especially as this was November and the weather was particularly overcast.

Each of these events required the adherence to certain protocols, one of which was that I must never attempt to set up the projector before the meeting was due to start, as you would in Britain. Rather, I had to wait until the host organisation's official electrician was present, so that he could make the necessary connections and switch on the room's fluorescent lights.

On this occasion he arrived with five minutes to spare before the 9.00 am start, as did almost all the 30 delegates, so I was anxious to have the equipment working and the room lit up immediately.

He quickly completed his duties, the power was on, the projector bulb lit up, and I was ready to start. Then sudden darkness; the power was off (it was exactly 9.00 am). The overhead projector bulb did not burst back into life, nor did the lights! The electrician then proceeded repeatedly to activate the various switches, perhaps thinking they were faulty and just needed a strong hand to operate them.

Nothing changed, except my blood pressure rose, as there was now a great deal of developing conversation, in Mandarin, about – presumably – why nothing was happening. I have to say this audience had not come willingly; they had been instructed to listen to me. I was beginning to sense this was not the most auspicious of starts.

The electrician went away, apparently to check the fuses to the room and the various circuits for the wall plugs. When he returned five minutes later, I learnt from my interpreter that there was no electricity to the whole building! I looked down the corridor to check this and then, for some reason, looked out of the window. In confirmation, I saw that no lights were on anywhere in the vicinity.

I assumed a power cut must have occurred.

Luckily, I had paper copy sets of the notes on the slides, which I then hurriedly distributed rather than at the end of the meeting, as was the usual format. With everybody supposedly on the same slide as me, I got the meeting started at about 9.15 am.

Imagine my surprise when, during the mid-morning refreshment break, the electrician and the manager of the building returned to the conference room. I was politely told, by my interpreter, that they had investigated the loss of electricity and learnt that the local government had ordered, at 9.00 am sharp, the redistribution of a quarter of the city's electricity supply to the Chinese national grid system.

This was because a decree had been issued by the central government in Beijing that the capital was to have all the electricity it needed because the wife of the President of the United States, Hilary Clinton, was leading an international women's conference in the Hall Of The People in Tiananmen Square.

In other words, there was to be no loss of electricity or service to such honoured guests – actually meaning no loss of face to the Chinese government – so anybody else nearby, like the residents of Tianjin, only four hours away, would just have to cope!

This last point really caught my attention because the building adjacent to the office I was in was a regional hospital. Its darkened windows certainly suggested they too didn't have any power, even from generators.

My interpreter suggested that any patient needing emergency treatment, perhaps even electrical resuscitation, was going to have to make do! Indeed, they would probably die so that the central government could present China in the best possible 'light'.

With that sobering thought in mind I carried on. Whilst the room was quite light during the morning and early afternoon, come late afternoon it got darker. I then distinctly observed many of the delegates at the back of the room beginning to nod off.

*I like to think it was because there was no electricity available to illuminate my presentation, rather than because of what I was actually saying!*

## IS IT REALLY YOU?

*The following anecdote is reproduced with the kind permission of*
*Roderick 'Rory' Keith Ogilvy Bremner FKC (born 6 April 1961). He is a Scottish impressionist*
*and comedian, noted for his work in political satire and impressions of British public figures.*

*He is also known for his work on Mock the Week as a panellist (for Series 1 and 2), award-winning show Rory Bremner … Who Else? and sketch comedy series Bremner, Bird and Fortune, which featured veteran comedians John Bird and John Fortune.*

In June 2009, during the first days of the UK's new coalition government, I travelled in a 'quiet' coach in a train from London to Manchester. I shared a table with three other passengers – two of us sat adjacent to the aisle and the other two next to the window. We each made pretence of getting our laptops out or reading the newspaper, certainly not talking to anyone at the table.

It wasn't until the refreshments trolley arrived, and the attendant asked what drink we would like, that the proverbial ice was broken. At this point, the passenger sitting to my right asked the person sitting diagonally across from him, 'You are Rory Bremner aren't you?'

I am sure the three of us, and the attendant, knew that it actually was the TV star and impersonator of British politicians and celebrities. However, without a moment's hesitation, he replied in an incredibly accurate and lifelike voice, 'No, I'm actually Tony Blair, the ex-Labour Prime Minister, travelling incognito.'

His delivery of this statement was so realistic that the attendant almost dropped the coffee she was serving into Rory's lap. In spite of the quiet, no talking rule, the three of us, and indeed some other passengers nearby, immediately burst out laughing. The remainder of the trip continued with much conversation about Rory's career and the pleasure his skill had given us all.

*Thanks Rory for making a trip so enjoyable and for making us laugh that day, as well as when watching your television shows.*

## IS THIS WHAT THEY MEAN BY RECYCLING?

In the 1960s, I led a student trip through North Africa to Libya and, while staying in Tripoli, we were graciously allowed to camp at a club that had a swimming pool. We had expected tummy upsets and had taken a very plentiful supply of toilet paper, but we were spared the anticipated indignities. As we were going to travel back by a more direct route through Italy, we offered our surplus toilet paper to the club manager but he perplexed us by asking, as he accepted it,

*'Has it been used?'*

## SPARKS REALLY DO FLY

If you have travelled the world, or even just in Europe, I'm sure that you, like me, have wondered why the electrical systems, especially sockets, can't be unified in some way. Why is it that French three-pin plugs will not fit German sockets, but they will fit Polish ones? German plugs won't fit French ones but they will fit sockets in Sweden and Greece and English plugs won't fit anywhere unless you definitely take an adapter!

The official answer to this unification question is that every country has its own historical rules regarding the distribution of electricity for portable appliances and lighting. Many different connection and lead cables are, therefore, needed to cope with the varying types of plugs, voltages and frequencies available to provide electrical power to gadgets like laptops.

Consequently, before the fairly recent invention of a single universal adapter that allows you to cope with such frustrations, those of us that travelled a lot (and at times in different countries consecutively) certainly needed to remember to carry the appropriate adapters with us. This was essential if you wanted to maintain power to your laptops, iPods and iPhones (especially as the battery life of these essential business tools seemed particularly short lived). We also needed to ensure we had the appropriate connecting cables as none of them seemed universal, instead, each fitted a particular gadget and nothing else.

At times, as I travelled the globe in my IT trouble-shooter role, I seemed to be carrying more cables and plugs than underwear. It was particularly embarrassing to have to expose all this technology (and my clothing) when there was a request to do so when the contents of my laptop rucksack triggered the x-ray machines at various airport departure terminals.

Whilst you can get a variety of adapters, and now the universal one, at airport gift shops and mainline train station newsagents, if you have ever left a cable back home, you soon realise that your gadget is last year's model – or even older – as these places only have the very latest equipment. The fact that you are then unable to connect (once the charge goes from your phone or computer) is not an excuse that goes down well with your boss, sitting at his comfortable head office desk.

When phoning back to explain my loss of power, it often seemed to me that, as much as the European Community 'Eurocrats' want us to get together, …

***… they don't in respect of having a 'Common Market' of electricity connections!***

## STOP THIEF! THAT'S MY CASE!

My friend's car port, at the front of his house, had direct access onto a busy main road. After parking his car, opening its boot and then carrying some items into his house, he inadvertently left his briefcase in full view of people passing by.

Imagine his shock when he returned and noticed somebody calmly walking away with his briefcase. When he shouted, 'Stop thief! That's my case!' the thief immediately started running, swerving to avoid pedestrians as he sped away.

My friend gave chase and, continuing to shout, this time using some expletives as well, he managed to gain on the thief. By now, they had both crossed over to the other side of the road, the single pavement switching sides at this point, and were continuing to run, one behind the other.

Just then, a car came alongside and my friend shouted, 'Please stop!' The driver promptly did, and my friend jumped into the passenger seat saying, just like something from a film, 'Follow that man!' The driver did just that until he was alongside the thief, whereupon my friend jumped out of the passenger seat and ran towards the front of the car.

However, at the same time, the robber turned and ran up the driver's side and climbed into the passenger seat behind him ... and the car sped away.

Imagine my friend's shock, and the amusement of several passers-by, who later, when unable to give the police much of a description of the thief, did say ...

**... both he and his driver had plenty of cheek!**

## THE BATHROOM FIGHTS BACK!

It had been a good summer evening in the old town of Schrobenhausen, Bavaria, drinking steins of beer with the customers and generally making merry. So, it was in a very mellow frame of mind that our small consultancy team finally retired to the family-run hotel where we were staying in the town.

Now, most hotels have a somewhat similar room layout and this was no exception. You entered through the door, past the bathroom and wardrobe, and on into the room.

During the night, one of my colleagues, affected by the beer, staggered out of bed and made his way to the bathroom. On entering, he felt around for the light, but then heard the door click shut behind him. 'That's odd,' he thought, but then his situation gradually became apparent. The problem he found himself with was that he was not in the bathroom, but out in the hotel corridor with no key, and worse, no pyjamas, and a locked door between him and his bed.

Unfortunately, at night the reception was unmanned so he had no one to let him back into his room and, when he moved in the corridor, the ceiling lights actuated, illuminating him in all his pristine glory.

As panic subsided a bit, he thought that he would knock and wake one of the team … the trouble was that he could not remember any of our room numbers with much certainty. A vision of knocking on a door and then being confronted by a very surprised total stranger, who at the sight of this night time display of manhood might be rather less than helpful, brought on another wave of panic. Luckily, the situation had such a sobering effect that a friend's bedroom number was remembered and he was admitted and spent the rest of the night on this room's floor.

Prior to our meeting with the customer the next day, his worries continued when we claimed to have got hold of a copy of the night security video tape from the hotel showing him in the corridor, and were going to include this with our project review PowerPoint presentation. Luckily, he made us change our minds as …

**… the reputation of British businessmen abroad was bad enough, without this embarrassment!**

## THINGS WERE DIFFERENT IN THE GOOD OLD DAYS

Once, when working in London, I arrived to find that I had left my office keys at home. Previously, if this had happened, I had worked on the content of my briefcase. But on that particular day, I needed some important papers from my desk.

Initiative was needed to get me out of an embarrassing situation, so I telephoned my wife who located the keys on the table by the front door of our home. She then placed them in a stout brown envelope, wrote my name on the front and drove quickly to the local train station.

There, standing at the front end of the platform, she asked the driver of a train going to Liverpool Street if he would hand them over to somebody who would be by the buffers of the platform at the end of his journey. He kindly agreed and, on arrival in London, undertook that action, passing the keys to my secretary who, with a taxi waiting outside the station entrance, returned to the office just in time for me to obtain the documents I needed.

*In today's health, safety and security conscious environment, I don't think such a gesture of kindness would be allowed, or even considered. Do you?*

## THREE TIMES, I'VE WONDERED TOO MUCH

There are times in life when you get yourself into a situation that is totally ridiculous and you wonder how on earth it happened. More importantly, how are you going to get out of it in one piece? Here are several that I've enjoyed (?):

### Oh, the shark has pearly teeth and he shows them shining white ...

Have you had a situation where you're snorkelling in warm, blue waters watching the cute little coloured fish, when all of a sudden you realise that a rather large, grey, pointy one is staring right at you and this fish is a barracuda! Of course, the first thing that happens is that you start hyperventilating, 'aha, aha, aha' ... which is not very useful.

Not feeling particularly confident you turn around to swim in the other direction when you realise that there is another barracuda, and another, and another, and so you do a bit more hyperventilating 'aha, aha, aha' ... and you start swimming towards them very fast to scare them away.

Unfortunately, the fish are not as frightened of you as you are of them so they stand their ground, proverbially speaking, and then ... they each open their mouths and show you rows of sharp, pointy teeth, all glistening white like in an advert for toothpaste.

*I first wondered, 'Oh dear,' and then, 'I might like a holiday at home next year!'*

### It's the landing that always hurts!

Perhaps you can also relate to climbing a small mountain and then suddenly slipping and falling off. Now, I can personally tell you that it's very odd that you don't ever remember the fall much but you do remember the landing!

'Doof' as you hit the ground, rucksack first, shortly followed by a gasp of pain as your ribs at the front try to reach the ribs at the back and, consequently, expel all the air from your lungs. After a second or two you attempt to suck down your first breath, only to scream instead, 'aghhhhh!'

**You lie there wondering why you got yourself into this situation.**

**How brave will I be?**

If, like me, you have enjoyed hiking in wild places (or at least ones where there aren't any street lamps shining), then you will know that there are certain decisions you have to make when you're sleeping rough.

Especially when, as you snuggle down into your sleeping bag and start watching the stars above and muse about the extraordinary planet we live on, you hear, 'Ooowwwww' – known as the call of the wild or White Fang, the wolf in the Disney nature films.

It's at this point that I wondered …

**… whether to keep my hands inside the sleeping bag or out – ready for a fight!**

## TUMMY PROBLEMS

In the late 1950s, I was travelling by car from Glasgow to the Isle of Skye, when I experienced a tummy upset. Reaching Fort William the situation became urgent and not knowing the town, I reckoned the railway station would be a safe bet for having toilets – they always were so equipped in those days.

We skidded into the station forecourt. I took little notice of the building-work going on as I rushed onto the platform and into the Gentlemen's toilet entrance where I found the anxiously anticipated heavy wooden cubicle doors with strong brass fittings, including a coin-operated door opening mechanism.

Relieved at making it, I placed my penny in the slot and pushed the door open. My relief turned to horror as all I could see were the open sky of the station yard and a full view of my wife sitting in our car.

**We have always thought it was cruel to demolish the toilets and leave the penny-in-the-slot doors in place.**

Postscript: At least there was a full sized door, even if no back wall. Unlike the toilets in Beijing station mentioned earlier.

## WHERE'S YOUR CUSTOMER COMPLAINT FORM?

Many years ago, I stayed in a West African hotel that had gone downhill since the days of its colonial splendour in the 1950s.

The information card in the room showed a tropically lush pool area and Caribbean style bar.

After a long day, the idea of a swim and cold beer was very appealing. I asked for directions and the receptionist explained the rather circuitous route.

On arrival, I found a broken pool with ten inches of green water and numerous frogs competing in their annual Olympics. The bar had long closed and been replaced with a rubbish tip and four 'free-range' chickens. I returned and complained to the receptionist who commented,

**'You didn't say you wanted to swim, Sir!'**

## 2)    *WAS IT SOMETHING THAT WAS SAID?*

Have you ever been in a situation where a careless or thoughtless phrase has been taken out of context, which has led to a major misunderstanding in a meeting, or been included in an email or Twitter message? We would be surprised if you have not. The stories that follow describe a spread of such experiences, both at work and play.

Readers may know that one of the most famous unfortunate reactions to something that was said was at the Charge of the Light Brigade. In the heat of battle, a misunderstood command 'to charge over there' sent 247 soldiers to their deaths in a very spectacular way.

I hasten to add that none of our contributors actually experienced that Victorian military disaster. I just mention it as a very unfortunate example of a situation (and comment) being misunderstood. The anecdotes in this chapter have more.

*Before then, some more newspaper headings, notices and thoughts ...*

TYPHOON RIPS THROUGH CEMETERY – HUNDREDS DEAD
*Did I read that right? Before or after the event?*

LADIES ARE REQUESTED NOT TO HAVE CHILDREN IN THE BAR
Seen on a wall behind a cocktail lounge in Lisbon

DROP YOUR TROUSERS HERE FOR THE BEST RESULTS
At a dry cleaners in Bangkok

PERSONS ARE PROHIBITED FROM PICKING FLOWERS FROM THEIR OWN GRAVES
Seen in a Dublin cemetery (not Transylvania)

WOULD YOU LIKE TO RIDE ON YOUR OWN ASS?
Advertisement for donkey rides at a fairground in Budapest

On the desk of an airline ticket office in Copenhagen:
WE TAKE YOUR BAGS AND SEND THEM IN ALL DIRECTIONS
*Reassuring or not?*

COFFEE TASTES BETTER IF LATRINES ARE DUG DOWN STREAM FROM AN ENCAMPMENT
American Civil War statement seen in the museum at Fort Du Pas in Florida

*How do you explain the oxymoron 'Now then' to French students learning the English language?*

Heard, in July 1992, as part of the safety briefing announcement on a flight on TAP, the national airline of Portugal, from Heathrow to Lisbon: 'If oxygen in the cabin fails, masks will fall from the ceiling lockers. As you pull them on – you all fall out.' Not quite what I, or the other passengers, wanted to hear as we would soon be flying at 30,000 feet.

INTERNATIONAL GREETINGS – THEM TO YOU

Have you ever had the experience of being driven away from an airport, at your overseas holiday destination, when the driver of the taxi kindly asks, 'Where are you from'? and you answer:

• 'London.' You then get the driver, a complete stranger, saying, 'Lovely Jubbly' as if you were a friend of Del Boy from the BBC television comedy show.

• 'Cardiff.' They try a Welsh accent, by saying, 'Yaki Da.'

• 'Edinburgh.' They try to impersonate Billy Connolly with, 'See you Jimmy.'

These greetings, a global approach in my experience, are invariably from taxi drivers hoping that such familiarity will increase the size of the tip you give them.

## AM I GETTING SOMETHING WRONG OR IS IT THE JOB?

While I was teaching French at a school for children with special needs, a few years ago, the whole school was summoned one day to the assembly hall to listen to the head teacher. Onto the stage, he invited a Year 10 boy who had secured a part-time job as a newspaper delivery boy. This was, in its way, remarkable and rather wonderful.

The head teacher explained to all the staff and pupils how hard it is to secure a paper round and that he was very proud of this pupil. I felt a sudden dig in the ribs from a pupil sitting at my side. 'Have you got a job, Miss?' Having taught this boy the rudiments of French for at least four years, I was rather astonished by his question, so I replied, 'Yes, I do have a job.'

The next question, asked without a hint of irony, was, 'Is it a paper round?'

*I wondered if he was trying to tell me something.*

## HAVE I HAD A HEART ATTACK OR JUST A SORE THROAT?

I studied French at school for five years and reached a sufficient level of incompetence to secure me a GCE 'O' level in the subject. However, it was not until we moved to France in 1989 that I realised just how pitiful my knowledge of the Gallic tongue was (as Mme Morris, my French teacher, called it).

Moving permanently to France, one realises fairly quickly that 'not everyone speaks English', and we were soon obliged to deal with the dreaded French 'administration' that uses every opportunity it can to send you away to avoid doing anything itself. We overcame difficulties with gas, electricity and telephone companies and became proficient imitators of the famous French Mime artist, Marcel Marceau, when we made visits to the local garage or hardware shop.

We chose Dr B as our family doctor because he was close by and because, according to our French neighbours, 'he speaks a little English'. (In fact, we have been going to him for 23 years now and the only English we have ever heard from his lips was, several years after our move when we took Scottish friends, needing emergency treatment, to him).

I went there fairly soon after our arrival, feeling a bit under the weather and he examined me. He then said 'Ne vous inquiétez pas, ce n'est qu'une angine,' which I translated as 'Don't worry yourself, it's only angina.' You can imagine my reaction to this news as my father had died from heart failure at the age of 51. My shocked look surprised Dr B somewhat.

Later, following some dictionary searching and discussions with my neighbours, I discovered that this 'angine' is their word for 'sore throat'. They also informed me that French was the language of diplomacy with no ambiguity, provided you used it correctly. (If I had been truly near death, he would have said 'Ce n'est qu'une angine de poitrine,' 'it's only angina!')

As he was only telling me that my throat was sore, I'd really no need to worry – funny, I thought …

*… that's not how my blood pressure was seeing things.*

## HELP, YOU'VE JUST SET MY 'EAR-HAIRS' ON FIRE!

Whilst working in 'downtown' Istanbul, and needing to be smartened up before an important business meeting, I visited a recommended gentlemen's hairdresser, only found in the maze of streets around the Grand Bazaar thanks to the display of the traditional red and white striped barber's pole positioned over the doorway.

After having been given a careful and professional haircut by, I assumed, the (elderly) owner of the shop – he was the only barber on the premises and everyone was waiting for his attention – I was, so it seemed, being asked, in Turkish, if I would also like my eyebrows, nostrils and ear-hairs trimmed. As I did not understand a word of this request, I just said, 'okay.' The careful use of scissors on the first two parts of my face then occurred and I sat back, relaxing in the chair whilst this activity was happening.

Imagine my surprise, if not horror, when, after a short pause, the barber turned towards me brandishing a lighted taper (looking like a long cotton wool bud), which he then proceeded to stick firstly into the cavity of my left ear, and then that of my right, before I could offer any sort of challenge or resistance!

A distinct smell of burnt flesh and hair enveloped my head, my ears certainly tingled and my brain went into overdrive wondering what he would do next.

Much conversation, again in Turkish, led to him liberally applying pleasant-smelling spirit to my hair and neck. When it reached inside my ears, my enjoyment (?) of the burning sensation I was still experiencing was certainly heightened.

Apparently, this is an old-fashioned method of finishing a haircut in Turkey.

**As I left the shop, I began to wonder if a descendant of Sweeney Todd, the Victorian fictional demon barber, was alive in Turkey and I'd had a lucky escape!**

## HOW NOT TO WIN BUSINESS IN TAIWAN

In Taiwan, my company's local agent spoke English and Mandarin Chinese. I spoke Dutch and English. The agent had an assistant who spoke Mandarin Chinese and the local Taiwanese dialect for the area, spoken by the customer we were visiting.

A simple question – in my Dutch mind – to open the conversation and, I hoped, start a fruitful discussion, came out of my mouth in English. 'Sir, how is your business doing today?' My agent then spoke this phrase, in Mandarin Chinese, to his assistant, who promptly then turned it into the local Taiwanese dialect of the customer. With that process in reverse, his answer came back to me as,

**'Yes, yesterday it was raining here too!'**

## I CALLED HIS TAXI THEN HIS BLUFF

One evening, in an infamous African city, I was in my 30-year-old taxi, which was made from varying parts of ten different Peugeots, when a policeman stopped it. He alleged that the driver had driven the wrong way along a street and, as I was a fare-paying passenger, I would have to pay an on the spot fine of $100.

The officer confirmed that I was legally the owner of this vintage wreck, so I asked the driver if he would like to earn $200. He readily agreed until I informed him that …

**… I required him to ship my newly prized classic car back to London!**

## I'D FORGOTTEN I DIDN'T LIKE SPIDERS

When I was a youngster, one of my best friends and I went to a holiday camp in the middle of a pine forest in southern England.

The chalets were not built very well, so many insects and 'creepy crawlies' found their way in. At that time of the year, the large hairy Harvest spiders were prevalent and literally hundreds invaded the chalet, so we spent the night with the bed sheets wrapped around our mouths to stop us swallowing any of them. It was an experience never to be forgotten.

Sometime later, the same friend and I went night fishing near to the road bridge that crosses the River Thames at Kingston-upon-Thames. In those days, there were disused oar huts by the riverside, which, whilst quite dilapidated, provided a roof over our heads if it rained. We always took our sleeping bags with us in case we wanted to avoid the rain, fish late into the night or have a sleep. This particular night, I got into my sleeping bag, and then my friend got into his.

As I put my head down I found a piece of old, much frayed rope, about two inches long, and threw it over my shoulder. It hit the ceiling of the hut and dropped down onto my friend's head. He immediately shouted, 'SPIDER, SPIDER,' and exited the hut, stumbling out, still in his sleeping bag.

I then watched him hop along the riverbank, as if taking part in a sack race, still shouting 'SPIDER.'

**The stupid thing was I leapt out too, having forgotten that it was only a piece of rope, not some rare type of eight-legged monster.**

## I'M DELIGHTED TO MEET A LADY OF THE NIGHT

It was suggested, whilst leading a major attitude survey interview programme with the entire management team of the largest insurance company in Portugal, that I learn Portuguese. This was both to be courteous to the executives and as a way of aiding my understanding of their feedback gained in the many interview meetings around the country.

I was privileged to be given language tuition by the client's own expert, a woman used to operating at the highest level in this company and with the Portuguese government. After a series of early morning one-hour sessions, she felt I was ready to take part in some of the lunchtime 'over-a-meal' dialogues that were part of this client's culture.

Joining such a group, including a board member and a very attractively dressed female executive, who I had briefly met at the start of the project, I addressed her in my new and best Portuguese.

I still recall the hilarious laughter of the entire group, my red-faced embarrassment and, luckily, her strong smile, as she turned to me and said, in perfect English, 'Thank you for asking but I am not a "Lady of the night".'

**I met her on many subsequent occasions and, each time, she assured me she still had not taken up the night-time occupation I thought she had had when we first met.**

## I ONCE KNEW SOME 'NICE WORKING GIRLS'

When I was a naïve teenager and working in Berkeley Square, London, one of the older guys in our office asked me if I had seen the prostitutes in Soho. I hadn't and, frankly, I didn't believe him as I often went there to buy sandwiches at lunchtime. However, I agreed to go with him so he

could point them out to me.

On approaching the area, he gestured towards three women who were standing on a corner and quietly said they were prostitutes. One was aged about 40 and the other two were about 20. They all looked very respectable, and the older one was holding some books. To me, it looked like an aunt and two nieces visiting a nearby bookshop, but my friend insisted we walk past them and, as we did, the older one propositioned us using some very colourful words, which I will not repeat.

### I was flabbergasted.

Some 20 years later, returning with a friend from a West End function, I suggested we went via the edge of Soho, en route to the underground tube station at Leicester Square. As we went along, I recounted this story, as we both knew the person who had originally brought me to this area. As we turned into the Soho area the same 40-year-old, albeit 20 years older, was standing on the same corner. I told my friend this and he thought I was making it up, so we went past her and she said exactly the same to me she as she had some 20 years earlier.

### He too was flabbergasted.

## I THINK WE'LL HOLIDAY AT HOME NEXT YEAR

Like us, Sally and Kahuure were employed at the Njoro Agricultural Research Station, situated on the western rim of The Rift Valley in Kenya, but, unfortunately, their Kenyan shillings were too rare and precious for them to afford a smart bungalow at the Keekorok Game Lodge. Thus, a night earlier, we had dropped them off next to a majestic tree in the Masai Mara Reserve and helped them set up their tent. Not one of those modern tents, mind you, but a colonial remnant made out of two bulky wooden A-frames and covered with a single piece of heavy canvas. The tree, we all thought, would provide shade. It was also a landmark, ensuring that next day we would find them and begin seeking out real lions.

When we returned in the morning, we did indeed find the tree – as well as bits and pieces from the tent. The good news was that we were clearly at the right place; the bad news was that Sally and Kahuure were nowhere to be seen!

We got back into the Land Rover and drove around the tree in a wide circle and past a dense area of shrubs some 50 metres away. There, hidden behind the tall shrubs, we were surprised to find a small cabin, with our friends waving at us from its doorway.

Once inside, they repeated their conversation of ten hours earlier:

Sally: 'Psst, Kahuure, do you hear that noise?'
Kahuure: 'I'm sleeping. What noise?'
Sally: 'Listen, there it is again … '
Kahuure: 'Oh that. Don't worry, those are antelopes mating.'
Sally: 'Really? Now, in the middle of the night?'
Kahuure: 'Trust me, I know Africa.'

They went back to sleep, but not for long. As fate would have it, we had pitched the tent right on the path of safari ants. Safari ants are a bit like a Roman legion: they travel fair distances in a long and dense formation, seeking out carcasses for a thorough cleaning before heading back 'rank and file' to their habitual abode. They mark their paths with scents, which keeps them from getting lost.

The tent was not an obstacle. Mind you, thanks to the casually hanging canvas, neither were our sleeping companions. As soon as the first ant bit, the rest followed, pheromonal trumpets co-ordinating the assault. Fighting and shaking off the persistent, gnawing little bugs, our friends jumped out of the tent.

That's when they saw the faint light of the nearby cabin, a solitary beacon of hope, and made a dash for it, screaming as they cut through the dense shrubs. Still hopping from one leg to the other in an attempt to shake off the last stubborn ants, they banged on the door until a kind soul finally opened it. The greetings were short and to the point:

'Who the $&#* are you and what are you doing here?' A rugged female doctoral student of wildlife biology pronounced the words in a New England accent. Then: 'Get in here, quick!'

After tending to their wounds and scratches, she invited Sally and Kahuure to look through a window. Uphill, some 300 metres away, was a herd of buffalos, not unlike mating antelopes, though ten to 20 times their weight. Masters in the art of the stampede, these creatures are avoided even by large lions and leopards. They were then invited to look out another window, towards the shrubs with the brand-new path courtesy of the ants. There, in plain sight, lay two lionesses tending to their cubs.

**Why they had not chosen to move moments earlier, as our two hapless tourist friends rushed past, remained both a mystery and a miracle.**

## MORE FUN FROM THE GOOD OLD DAYS

Before the Second World War (in an age more innocent than now), this trick was commonly played on any new, unsuspecting apprentices as they began their career on our Essex arable farm. When they were on fields some considerable distance from the barns and central workshop, they would each be asked to walk back there to find a bubble for the spirit level being used, to check that the ploughing was level!

***Needless to say, after two lengthy walks – there and back – such apprentices never fell for that request twice!***

Note: Please read 'I requested a Long Weight' in Chapter 4 to learn of another trick played on an innocent new worker.

## NOW I KNOW WHAT RETIRED PEOPLE TRY TO DO EACH DAY

Before I took early retirement, I had often asked myself how retired people filled their days. Recently becoming one of them, and able to concentrate on my family, hobbies and the fact that I didn't have to get up at five each morning to commute to London, I began to find I was doing a wide range of interesting things and – like so many others – wondering 'how did I ever manage to find time to go to work?'

Particularly, I began to enjoy using the, free to pensioners, Park-and-Ride bus to our local town centre and it was on one of these days that I found myself standing alongside the front of a car parked definitely where it shouldn't be – straddling two yellow lines outside the public conveniences!

Whilst I was thinking how brave the owner of the car must be to leave it in such a position, a traffic warden walked up to the front of the vehicle and began writing out a parking ticket. I turned to him and said, 'Excuse me, but perhaps the owner of the car needed to use these facilities,' pointing to the toilets.

Assuming the car was mine, he carried on placing the ticket underneath the windscreen wipers. I said, 'That's a bit b******y officious,' at which point he began to write another one telling me that I should not make such comments to a council official.

Then he noticed that the vehicle's tax had expired so that became the reason for a third ticket.

By now, this petty bureaucrat had been kept busy for over ten minutes. Personally, I didn't care. I felt that, now I'd retired, it was important I tried to talk with some of the people I met, especially as I've found it's important to live by the adage from the Reader's Digest magazine:

**A little humour helps you live a long life!**

## TEAMWORK, ALCOHOL AND ME

Teamwork did not come easily to me. I was a 'quiet type', prone to reading and thinking, but with an inner determination looking for a way out. I was always envious of those of my contemporaries who were natural born organisers and leaders. To get from that point to globetrotting for high tech companies was an evolutionary process, not without its moments.

My earliest recollection of leading a team was being promoted to Acting Patrol Leader for the Pigeon Patrol of my local Scout Troop, on the occasion of a competitive evening navigation exercise in Epping Forest on the outskirts of London. My first act of folly was to appoint, over the heads of more experienced patrol members, my younger brother as my Assistant Patrol Leader, and then to set off into the dusk to try to find the various checkpoints but without much forward planning. After several stops to take stock of progress and review our direction of travel, I was persuaded that we were both lost and late. When we stumbled across a track known to the more experienced patrol members, we made a beeline for the finish. Naturally, we arrived last of all the patrols by a substantial and, as we subsequently learnt, legendary margin.

Some years later, I had slightly more success as one of a team of two students on our inaugural trip to the USA. Although our vacation contacts were largely arranged by my father, once we'd arrived, it was Dave, my student friend, with his suave good looks, natural charm and confidence, who was in the vanguard of our social encounters. At the end of our six week vacation job in the Wayne Gasket Company, we told Annie, our larger-than-life Italian-American landlady and her other lodger, John, the same age as us, that we would be back to collect our bags directly after work and then head off to the downtown bus station to catch the Greyhound bus to Chicago at 10.30 pm that night. That was the plan.

On the last day, we had decided that rather than waste perfectly good clean clothes, which were ready for our extended sight-seeing travels around the US, we would wear our 'pre-worn' work attire. For my part, I donned a mildly grubby nylon shirt, which passed the nose test at an arm's length, and off we set. The morning went quickly. Just before the time of our half hour lunch break, the company's President (a friend of my father's) came to tell us he had decided we were going out to a farewell lunch with him at his 'club'. This turned out to be a decidedly up-market bar for executives, who were attended to by an unending stream of waitresses whose uniforms consisted of tight blouses, fishnet tights and short skirts.

Our embarrassment at our inappropriate attire was soon dulled by alcohol and our exceptionally hospitable host and his friends. We returned from our long lunch, exuding bonhomie, and perambulated unsteadily around the factory in the remains of the afternoon, saying our goodbyes. Come 4.00 pm, we sought a lift from Bill, our foreman, to go directly back to our lodgings instead of Bar 7 for our normal end-of-day beer. However, Bill insisted we would stop off there for a farewell drink and, as he was driving, our protests were ineffective. Naturally, being Friday, Bar 7 was busier than usual and, having been 'softened up' by our lunchtime session and then by a farewell drink from Bill, we found it futile to resist the offer of further drinks from everyone else present.

Well into the evening, Hank, 'the mad Dutchman', also from the factory, arrived. Although it was obvious he had already had a few, he loudly insisted that Bill was too drunk to drive us back to our lodgings and, after a few more parting drinks all round, Dave and I fell into Hank's car and off we meandered.

'I'm glad I've got you to myself at last,' Hank announced. 'I am now going to take you to my favourite bar for a farewell drink.' I recall we arrived there feeling decidedly the worse for wear. Eventually, after a 'decent interval' propping up the bar, Hank heeded our pleas that we had had 'elegant sufficiency' of liquid beverage, and agreed to take us 'home'.

In the early hours, we proceeded in the general direction of our lodgings, but the nearer we got, the more Hank failed to understand simple directions. His skill to drive in a straight line was lost. More by luck than judgement, we eventually found ourselves in the next street to our house, where we 'alighted' to watch Hank speed off, weaving his way into the distance.

Luckily, Dave had recognised where we were and could see Annie's house, with a light in the window, across a large field. I could not focus on anything beyond our immediate surroundings. Dave, on the other hand, was incapable of standing unaided.

Teamwork: Remember me mentioning teamwork? Taking the motto 'Strength through alcohol' to heart, I carried Dave like a baby directly across this unmade ground in pitch darkness, stumbling on unseen hazards, including a barbed wire fence, with Dave giving directions whenever his head happened to catch sight of our goal. We made it! Bursting in through the door we found Annie, who, worried sick about her charges, had sent lodger John out in an attempt to track us down in likely haunts in Detroit.

Having failed, they had both (in their opinion) taken the next best course of action, which was to drown their sorrow at losing us by hitting hard liquor! To celebrate our safe return, they made us join them, this time sharing more than a few bottles of beer, as well as the liquor. Very, very slowly the next morning we tried to recover the use of our faculties, drinking our version of the 'Hair of the Dog' – milk and ice cubes. Annie's scornful comment was soon ringing in our ears.

*'God, I've never seen milk drunk on the rocks before.'*

## THANK GOODNESS I KEPT MY HEAD

Many African police officials survive on money they fleece from motorists by stopping them and pointing out that they are breaking certain laws, most of which do not exist. The existence of a white westerner in the passenger seat often increases the fines levied.

Not many people I know can boast about being 'fined' for not having a mobile sanitation licence, nor, of not having paid a 'decapitation tax'!

*The very wording of the latter, however, persuaded me to pay up without delay!*

## THE SCHOOL REPORT SAID 'MUST TRY HARDER' – SO WE DID!

The need for more parental involvement was highlighted in our OFSTED report following an inspection that had put the school, I had recently become head teacher of, into 'special measures', ie we had failed to meet an acceptable standard of education for our pupils.

The school was situated in an area of high social deprivation and served many vulnerable families, so to start to develop a good home/school relationship it was decided to set up a 'Friends of the School' group. The initial meeting to seek support for this initiative was very encouraging and a committee was formed with nominations for Chair, Secretary and Treasurer accepted.

A committee meeting was arranged to set the agenda for forthcoming meetings. At this point, the Chairperson whispered that she was too shy

to stand up in front of a group of parents and speak because she would 'die of embarrassment'. The Secretary then wished to find out exactly what her role would be as she could not read or write, but would do her best to remember what was said. At this point, someone noticed that the mum nominated for Treasurer was not present. 'Oh, she has just been arrested at Tesco's for shoplifting, so can't make it today,' stated another mum.

**As head teacher, I suddenly realised we needed more support than we had originally thought.**

Postscript: Notwithstanding the above, The Friends of the School did thrive, supporting many school initiatives, raising thousands of pounds for the school, with OFSTED later recognising parental involvement in their children's education as outstanding. Achievements that made us all very proud.

## THIS HOTEL OFFERED SOMETHING QUITE DIFFERENT FROM LOYALTY POINTS!

In the middle of a winter, many years ago, my company sent me to Korea. There was a shortage of hotels and so I was placed in an establishment described as the 'Tourist Hotel'.

Whilst the meals were of a good standard, breakfast was always a surprise with nothing recognisable except 'eggy' toast. Bedrooms were huge and the plumbing made a good attempt at working most of the time. There was only one problem: the temperature of the hotel – it was freezing. At meals everyone was dressed in several layers; all that seemed to be missing were gloves.

Trying to get warm in bed seemed impossible, no matter how many clothes were worn. Others did not seem concerned about the cold in bed, which I could not understand until I checked out after a week or so. At the reception desk, going through the bill, we agreed on the number of nights and the restaurant and bar charges, but what we could not agree upon was how many people were in my room. I insisted it was only me, but the hotel would not believe me.

It took some time before the penny dropped; the hotel had found a way to keep their guests warm at night. They would kindly arrange for someone to share your bed and keep you warm at night.

It was apparently normal for guests at this hotel to use this special warmth service, so common in fact, that staff had not thought to mention it to me when I checked in.

**If only I had known, I might have been warmer but I don't think I would have told my company or my wife once back home!**

## YOU LIKE A GOOD TIME – ANY TIME?

On a business trip to Moscow, I had been booked into an old Russian Intourist hotel (something I should have avoided). I had a bed, if you can call an old flea-ridden mattress on a plank of wood a bed, an old green telephone, a hole in a wall for a shower, and a single overhead light that did not work, so I had to use matches to see my way around the darkened room.

At midnight, the phone started ringing – 'Mr, Mr, you like pretty woman?' to which I replied, 'No thanks' and slammed the phone down.

Every hour the phone would ring with the same broken English phrase asking if I wanted someone to spend the night with me. As I was tired, I wasn't very polite with my responses – they just didn't understand 'No!'

The last call came at 4.00 am when they changed tack – this time with 'Mr, Mr, you want a young boy?' After swearing at them, and to make sure the phone would not ring again for me, or probably any future guests …

**… I pulled the telephone cord out of the wall!**

## YOU'LL NOT CATCH ME A SECOND TIME!

My father often told the story of his first efforts at ploughing on the family farm. This was back in the 1920s and the days of horse-drawn ploughs, so some knowledge of horsemanship was certainly needed.

One day an elderly but very experienced ploughman accompanied my father and, together, they led the horse off down the field. When the animal, of some height, weight and strength, reached the end, my father wanted him to stop and so naturally, he called out, 'Whoa, whoa.' (Stop, stop.)

He stopped, right on one of my father's feet!

Naturally, he called out, saying, again, 'Whoa, Whoa!'

Unfortunately, the horse just stood there, his weight pressing down on my father's young and tender foot.

After a few more pleas from my father for the horse to stop standing on his foot, his elderly companion, who had obviously seen it all before during many years of working on the farm, said calmly, in his broad Essex accent, 'When you've had enough boy, just say "gee-up".' (Move on.)

He did and, sure enough, the horse began to walk smoothly away as my father hopped about with tears streaming down his face.

**Needless to say, he never used the wrong command again!**

## 3) *WAS IT SOMETHING THAT WAS EATEN OR DRUNK?*

In these trusting times of international cuisine and fast food burgers, with or without the scandal of horsemeat being served instead of prime beef, the phrase coined in the 20th century, 'You are what you eat' could not be more relevant to us now living in the third millennium.

Perhaps there are some readers who can recall the after-effects of a not quite delicious meal or a hangover 'hanging-over' too long? On the other hand, have you used – or been the recipient of – a meal or a drink to reinforce or even affect the outcome of a business meeting or social engagement, or to 'oil the wheels of love'?

Hopefully, all your memories are happy ones and not just of a dodgy curry regurgitated during your student days.

*Newspaper headings and notices about things to avoid (or not?)*

NEW STUDY OF OBESITY LOOKS FOR LARGER TEST GROUP
*Weren't they fat enough already?*

KIDS MAKE NUTRITIOUS SNACKS
*I wonder what they taste like – chicken?*

In an advertisement for a Swiss restaurant:
CHOOSING OUR WINES LEAVES YOU NOTHING TO HOPE FOR

In a small café in the East End of London:
OPEN SEVEN DAYS A WEEK AND WEEKENDS
*I knew Londoners worked hard but this is stretching things too far*

In a Thai bar:
SPECIAL COCKTAILS FOR THE LADIES WITH NUTS
*(I'd heard of lady boys but never met one)*

Thought: To paraphrase a quote by James Michener, American Author and Pulitzer Prize winner, 'If you reject the food, ignore the customs, fear the religion and avoid the people you might be better off staying at home.'

'THOSE PENCILS LOOK STRANGE'
The sentiments in Michener's quotation came to mind as I remembered viewing street cooking in China. It always provided an interesting insight into what can be cooked and served – apparently, everything under the moon and sun!

Anyway, late one Saturday evening, I really had to reject the offer of eating, at a Chinese pavement vendor's stand, what was on a dinner plate resting on a brazier lying on the pavement. Perhaps it was their appearance as wooden pencils that put me off, or, <u>more likely</u>, it was learning that 'the fried and battered wooden pencils' were actually chicken penises laid out straight and fried to perfection (?) as tasty nibbles.

## AN ALL-YOU-CAN-EAT BREAKFAST – CHINESE STYLE

I hope you enjoyed the fog story that began this collection, the one behind the book's title mentioning the visit of the Chinese government officials to the UK. You will recall that it was the first time they had left the Chinese mainland and come west …

… Well, once they were safely checked into their hotel rooms, and before they had a light buffet supper, I made some brief announcements, including the fact that breakfast the following morning would be available from 7.30 am and our first session, a group photograph, would take place at 9.30 am sharp. I stressed they should not be late for either event.

Imagine my surprise next morning when, by chance, I noticed that **all** 30 guests were lined up outside the entrance to the hotel's dining room at 7.25 am. I had been expecting them to dribble in during the 90 minutes that had been allocated as their breakfast time.

No matter, I already knew the dining room was prepared and the food counters were amply stocked with all the ingredients to ensure both Chinese dishes and a Full English cooked breakfast were available, so I asked the staff to open the doors and invite the guests in exactly on time.

As they did so, my two interpreters explained that the cereals were at the first long table, other help-yourself items in the centre and then all the hot dishes were available from the two chefs at the last, and main, serving counter. Here, I had already noticed that the bacon, beans, black pudding, eggs, sausages, mushrooms and tomatoes looked particularly appetising and I was certainly ready to enjoy them.

Imagine my alarm when I realised that the people at the head of the queue had begun to move from the first counter, each holding a large dinner plate containing cereals and fruit, to the middle one, where items from a continental buffet were also placed on the same plate, and were now arriving at the hot food counter where all the ingredients of a Full English were being loaded on top of the food they had already selected.

I also noticed that the hot food had begun to slide about on the cold cereals and milk that were, obviously, underneath.

Panicking, I urgently asked my interpreters to speak to everyone and reassure them that they could have as many products for breakfast as they wished – after all, we'd got 90 minutes to sit and eat it all – it was just not our English custom to have everything at once, and certainly **not** on the same plate.

I was pleased to note that those further down the queue took note of this suggestion as they then selected individual items and made many return trips to the tables and serving counter.

It later transpired that, whilst they had eaten on the plane as it flew from Beijing, food had last been served almost 25 hours earlier. Also, the previous evening's supper was enjoyed – but it was far too delicate for their appetites. They were, therefore, now very hungry.

Most importantly, I was told, and I learned from my own experience of living in their country, hot dishes, once served, needed to be eaten quickly as they were always prepared quite some distance away from tables in the dining rooms of the government offices in which the staff were based. To me, rice, if eaten cold, was like enjoying a British rice pudding alongside your meat or fish dish.

*Often, a combination, I would find out later, my digestion could not properly enjoy.*

## CORDON BLEU? I DON'T THINK SO

On the wine list in an Indian restaurant in Guyana, I spotted Jacobs Greek: a fine and rare wine that might have been particularly good with the Vegetarian Chicken, Vegetarian Duck, Vegetarian Lamb and Vegetarian Fish at a Chinese eatery not too far away.

*However, I didn't try these 'vegetarian' dishes, which might be in breach of the Trade Descriptions Act!*

Also in an Indian restaurant, at the end of the meal, the waiter brought some small white discs on a plate, which resembled plain white after-dinner mints. He proceeded to pour a little water onto them and they grew, first into small cylindrical marshmallows, then they expanded to become sheets of soft paper. Unfortunately, one of the guests, missing this action, had already popped what he assumed was a mint into his mouth …

*… only to discover that he had a small paper towel sticking out from between his lips.*

A menu in Poland boasted tough cheese and a dish they called 'chicken in the after-grass'. Another favourite is 'pigeons'. However, these never flew …

*… but were a tasty mixture of mincemeat and rice wrapped in a cabbage leaf.*

In the mid-1990s, a senior official from one of the countries seeking to join the EU was over in Brussels for a meeting. The table had been prepared with starters already laid out, but right in front of the official's place there was a jar of mayonnaise. He proceeded to unscrew the top and gobbled up the whole jar!

*Nobody dared to point out to him the error of his ways, but later on his stomach probably did.*

## EMBARRASSED BY A 'BIG MAC' IN BEIJING

Working in China, in 1995, I went to Tiananmen Square, Beijing to celebrate with my Chinese interpreter, his wife and daughter, the most important time in the annual calendar of the People's Republic of China: the founding of the nation by Chairman Mao Zedong on 1 October.

As we arrived in the square, I realised that it lived up to its claim to be the largest, city centre, public square in the world. It covers an area of 44 hectares – 500 metres in width and 880 metres in length – and can accommodate 1,000,000 people – all of whom seemed to be there with me that day.

I'm proud to report that being six feet tall, I seemed to be looking over the heads of most of the Chinese holidaymakers. It was then that I also noticed that there were very few other Europeans present for, at that time, Western Tour companies dissuaded their customers from visiting the area because they knew it would be almost entirely filled with Chinese!

However, our visit was not only to the square but also to surrounding sites like the Great Hall of the People, The Palace Museum (aka The Forbidden City) and the biggest McDonald's restaurant in the World.

This was located at Wangfujing, in a road adjacent to the top left corner of the square and directly opposite – in the distance – the Meriden Gate of the Palace. It took some time for us to push our way to that location and then observe that there was a very long queue of expectant diners. Not surprising, as it seated 700 people! Before joining them, my 'host' made sure we were given our waiting-tickets. They were like those you now get at various counters in supermarkets.

These were an attempt to ensure everyone queued quietly and in sequence. We almost did.

Entering the restaurant, he ordered our food then, at the same time, told his wife and daughter to find somewhere for us to sit. This looked impossible. Not to them. They proceeded to stand behind a family that was already occupying a table – and I had to do the same. I was then told to lean over the diners!

Seeing a European on that day was already a rare sight in the square. Having the only one in the restaurant hovering behind you was also something different, so this group of frightened diners – with much shouting in Mandarin, which luckily I did not understand – got up and pushed their way past us. In a flash we three – yes, including me, but very embarrassed – had sat down on the warm seats, just in time for my interpreter to deliver our food, saying,

**'I knew they'd move once they saw you!'**

Note: You may remember the London underground story in Chapter 1. Another example of a British traveller being embarrassed abroad!

## ENJOY THE MEAL? YES, AND THE COMPANY OF THE TRAY IT WAS ON!

Shortly after I took off on a long-haul flight, the cabin crew came round to serve lunch. I unfolded the drop-down tray and pulled it towards me. Normally the tray should stop – but mine didn't, it kept coming right off the sliders! Balancing one's meal on one's lap is one thing, but then having to stow the tray down the side of the seat …

**… is surely a breach of air travel regulations but the cabin crew didn't seem to worry!**

## HAVE YOU TRIED OUR FLYING BEER?

Travelling on a small, 12-seat propeller plane from Edinburgh to Aberdeen in 1990, in the days leading up to Christmas when everyone just 'wanted to get home', we were made to wait anxiously for the plane to be de-iced before it could take off in a snow storm. On boarding, we were invited to take a can of Newcastle Brown ale from a cool box, just inside the cabin doorway. (Apparently, this was the only in-flight refreshment service.)

Approaching the runway at Aberdeen, in the same storm, we then 'enjoyed' our plane suddenly and violently veering off its flight path.

Through the windscreen, we watched, with horror, an airliner loom unexpectedly in front of us.

Not all was lost, as this evasive action meant we benefited from a second pass over the city below, albeit at almost right angles to the ground. Of course, as we banked for the successful attempt at landing, the empty, or almost empty, beer cans went flying of their own accord!

On arrival, as we wiped ourselves down and left the plane, the pilot said calmly, 'Phew that was a near miss.'

**Descending the stairs and almost kissing the ground, we all agreed!**

### I'M NOT SURPRISED YOU'RE ILL

In 1978, I was working for the Daily Telegraph in Washington. Most of the time I was covering Congress, the Pentagon, the State Department and, if I was lucky, the White House, but every so often I got out of town.

That summer, a really interesting assignment came my way: a NATO press trip to Fort Bragg in North Carolina, home of the famous Green Berets. Some of these paratroopers laid on demonstrations to show how much they had learned since Vietnam. These included a display of unarmed combat 'with lethal blows omitted', a psychological warfare operation, which consisted of loudspeakers blasting out 'Come out, you're surrounded!' in Russian, and an exercise in building shelters for survival behind enemy lines – and animal traps which looked remarkably similar, though a little smaller. An Australian SAS officer with us commented that it all showed how little they had learned rather than how much, but at their passing-out parade we were all moved by the tears of their senior instructor, who was retiring.

The animal traps were there for a purpose. The Green Berets had been out on a 24-hour exercise to prepare them for operating behind enemy lines and they were expected to live off the land. When it was over, they served up for us a lunch of the wildlife they had trapped. We had tea made from sassafras roots (bearable), and a giant Hispanic sergeant prepared us possum, fox and frog, cooked on a wood fire and served in foil. The frog tasted like chicken, the possum was stringy and the fox revolting but, in the best tradition of investigative journalism, I went through the card – then telephoned an enthusiastic article back to the Telegraph.

Straight after the press trip, I was due back in London to start a holiday.

No sooner had I arrived than I went down with salmonella of the most dramatic variety. For three days I was too weak to leave the house. When eventually I crawled to the doctor's and he asked what I had been eating, I told him: 'Possum, fox and frog.'

*All he could say was: 'I'm not surprised you're ill.' I have not eaten wildlife since.*

## ISN'T THAT WHAT A FRIDGE IS FOR?

Visiting a Zambian village as part of my missionary support work, I was invited into the headman's home and, as a courtesy, invited to share his family's meal.

On looking round his very clean accommodation, which from the outside was just a circular, thatched building, I couldn't help but notice the many joints of fresh and old meat hanging from the ceiling of his mud-hut. A large and bright white refrigerator, powered by a small, quiet, generator, standing in a sort of serving area, also caught my eye.

Later, as I ate the delicious stew, I wondered how many of the flies, similar to the ones I could now see flying above my head, had landed on the joints of meat and were now also in the mixture.

I thanked him for his hospitality and politely asked, 'Why don't you keep the meat in the fridge?' He answered that the fridge was already in use and proceeded, with a flourish, to open its door and show me – with great pride – that it was completely full of a well-known brand of bottled beer!

*In a land of much heat, it was obvious that he had decided what his priorities were!*

## NOT SURE THIS RESTAURANT WILL ALLOW ME BACK A THIRD TIME

I took my wife and my two young children to dinner in a restaurant in Alameda, near Lisbon in Portugal. As my Portuguese was almost non-existent, I asked the waiter to describe a dish that we were reading about on the menu. I knew it said something about being a fish dish but not much else.

Without a moment's hesitation, he walked over to another diner who was obviously enjoying his meal, picked up his plate (it was actually the dish I was enquiring about), brought it to me and said, in very poor English, 'This is what it is!'

My wife and children were stunned into silence by this action. So too was the guest whose meal had been borrowed for my examination!

Returning to the same restaurant later in the week, my wife ordered a fresh crab dish that was advertised – in English (perhaps for our benefit) – on the 'specials board'.

When after some time it arrived, she was very surprised to be served a large, but luckily, completely cooked crab, still in its shell.

She was then provided with a strong-looking hammer and a slab of marble and invited to crack open the shell and large, fearsome looking, claws. She did this with gusto (perhaps the fine Portuguese wine was already working its spell), sending the fragments of the crustacean all over the other diners sitting at adjoining tables.

By coincidence, two of them had been there during our earlier visit and I think they began to say to each other, something like,

### *'How strange these English tourists are ...'*

## ONE FOR THE ROAD, RUSSIAN STYLE

On arriving at Sheremetov Airport for the twentieth time in a couple of years, I went straight to the factory for negotiations on the latest tender. Two colleagues and I worked all day on various adjustments to our pricing offer and, eventually, managed to secure the contract.

Thereafter, it was customary to have an evening meal and some vodka with the customers and socialise. This was always a good night and we all thoroughly enjoyed ourselves. However, the customers left at 1.00 am and then someone mentioned we should have 'one for the road', the effects of Russian vodka having already cemented our belief that this was the 'done thing'. The next thing we knew it was 4.00 am and we found ourselves in some rough bar with cigars held in our hands; we did not even smoke. At this stage, the internal flight, to the location of another customer, looked unlikely, especially as it was due to leave at 6.30 am.

A quick exit into a taxi and swift change into the suit at the hotel room resulted in the zip slider on the front of my trousers flying off, thus leaving them open and that area of my clothing underneath rather exposed. Anyway, there was no time to waste and I threw the suit jacket on to cover up the obvious gap.

Flying south some distance resulted in a rather large jump in temperature. This, coupled with the effects of the previous night, was making the journey rather uncomfortable. On arrival at the customer's factory, the sweat was pouring out, as well as the alcohol. The factory manager insisted I relax and take my jacket off, but for obvious reasons I declined and battled on through.

I managed to secure another order and made my way back to the airport and Moscow. On my arrival at 11.00 pm, some colleagues were in the restaurant, about to tuck into their steak and chips. One of them thought I looked so hungry and worn out that he passed me his plate of steak and chips that had just been served. Thanking him profusely, I did not wait for him to change his mind but instead gratefully tucked in.

**The moral of a business trip like this? Avoid drinking with the Russians, especially their vodka, and don't ever travel 'Commando Style'.**

## POLISH OR POTATOES?

Do you, like me, get anxious on hearing a fire alarm bell? My reaction is based on instantly remembering my time at Aborfield Barracks in Berkshire, having been sent to its Radar Training school, and its fire-fighting equipment. This was a petrol-driven fire pump that was housed in a shed near the main entrance.

During the working day, this appliance (for that is the technical name for a fire-pump) would be hitched onto the back of a Land Rover by the permanent staff of the camp. If needed for an emergency, it could then be easily driven to the fire, connected to a hydrant, and used to help tackle the blaze until the local civilian fire engine arrived. If not, everyone seemed, at one time or another, to be polishing it before it was returned to its shed at the end of each afternoon. However, for evenings and weekend cover there was a team of two lance corporals and six privates detailed from the 'students' each week. This team was not allowed to leave the camp for the whole week and had to parade by the shed every evening. Whilst there, they pulled the pump outside and practised running out a hose.

After this drill, the pump was pushed back into its shed and two men were detailed to – wait for it – once again, polish the brass fittings! Meanwhile, the rest of the fire brigade squad, who could not leave camp anyway, was marched to the cookhouse to peel all the potatoes needed for the next day's meals.

Luckily, I never had to face a real blaze but there was an apocryphal story about a real fire one night. The fire alarm sounded. Everyone turned out and formed up on the square for a roll call.

In came the three armed policemen

However, no one went near the fire pump to drag it over to the fire, unroll the hoses and tackle it as expected.

So the fire continued to burn merrily until the civilian fire engine turned up.

Only later were all the 'fire team' discovered in the cookhouse, having rushed inside to peel even more potatoes. Volunteering to do this meant they had kept the pump clean, thereby…

### *… avoiding the need to polish it yet again!*

## SOBERING UP QUICKLY IN BANGKOK

I had recently moved from the UK to Bangkok, Thailand as an English teacher, along with Alex, one of my best friends from home, when we found ourselves out 'on the town' and in a local club called 'Booze'. There we drank Chang, a strong local beer, and proceeded to show the Thais how the Brits can really 'boogie on down' on the dance floor.

Enjoying ourselves immensely, the time was flying by when, suddenly, the music stops and all the lights come on. Standing on the club's stage is someone dressed in a Thai police uniform. I say, 'Hey up Alex seems like they've got a little show for the ladies,' truly expecting the 1980s hit song Y-M-C-A to start.

Our more experienced friends had other ideas and told us to vacate the premises immediately. A little confused about what was happening, we nevertheless rushed for the exit, but about 12 Thai policemen, with guns and not looking too friendly, were already blocking it. Not understanding the situation, I decided to ask one of them what was going on and was duly told, 'You p**s now, no escape!'

The police then proceeded to line everyone up outside the toilets with the view of making us all pee in a cup (not at the same time mind, and not the same cup), then testing it for any drugs that may have been consumed, a crime heavily punishable in Thailand. I did not have any real worries on that score. What concerned me more was that the club only had one toilet and over 300 people waiting to use it – and even more worrying, I had to be at school in the morning and it was already quite late. My new friends also informed me that we would be expected to show our passports to the police unless we wanted to sleep on a jail cell floor for the night. Mine was sitting on my bedroom desk. Things were looking grim!

After waiting in line for about ten minutes without any progress, Alex and I decided to try walking out the exit as if we had already been tested OK. Unfortunately, while they believed my good friend's story, I was sent to the back of the queue! After more anxious standing in line, and desperately wanting to use the toilet after consuming all those Chang beers, a Thai copper randomly grabbed me from the group of expats I was with and pushed me towards the exit door.

He shouted, 'You show passport now!' I gulped hard, grabbed my wallet and showed him the only form of ID I had on me, which happened to be an expired student union card from my time studying in Brisbane, Australia; not ideal. Three police officers then gathered round to stare at the old card for what seemed like an eternity and then finally asked, 'You Ryan John?' 'Yes,' I replied. 'OK, you go now. Welcome to Thailand Ryan John.'

Welcome indeed! Shocked, with no clue of what just happened and no desire to inquire, I finally made it home by 3.00 am. With just three hours' sleep, I was back teaching my first class of the day. From then on I always carried my special student union card …

**… just in case I needed to baffle the police once again.**

Postscript: I also made sure I never again drank too many Chang beers whilst I was in Bangkok!

## WAS THE PROBLEM MARIANNE'S SWEET TOOTH – OR SOMETHING ELSE?

Some years ago, a Swedish friend of mine, Marianne, was working in Ireland for a few months, improving her English along the way.

One day, at a meal with friends, they reached the dessert course. Keen to sample the local, traditional dishes Marianne ordered the apple pie. Asked if she would prefer ice cream or cream with her pie she firmly said, 'Oh no, I would like mustard.' 'Mustard dear?' asked the waitress. 'Are you quite sure?' Marianne remained resolute: 'Definitely, I'd like some mustard please.'

The waitress tried a couple of times more to get her to accept ice cream or fresh cream before giving in, looking skywards (probably thinking 'who can account for the tastes of foreigners – this must be some quaint Scandinavian delicacy') and walked off to fetch the desserts.

**Later, as her taste buds were challenged, Marianne realised that the word she should have used was 'custard'.**

## DO YOU LIKE TO EAT 'TOY-TOISE'?

In 1997, as a thank you for successfully completing the management employee part of a five-year World Bank development project, I was given the honour of a farewell banquet by Mr Lin, the fourth Mayor of Tianjin.

This was held in a restaurant he particularly liked for the quality and range of its cuisine and wines. Its main conference hall had been set out with ten tables, with 12 people on each, as well as a top table for me as key guest, the World Bank executives, my team colleagues and our respective Mandarin language translators.

As you may know, politicians in this country are highly skilled at public speaking and crowd motivation, as well as being charming but shrewd operators in terms of ensuring they have many friends in the business and civil service community. So, with some of those wines, Chinese gin and beers already on the tables – and being enjoyed – I was 'hand-clapped' a welcome into this auspicious event by the Mayor, encouraging his guests to follow his fine example.

I was not allowed to sit down, but rather made to stand on the right side of the Mayor with my interpreter close behind me. Then, after some stirring and patriotic announcements by Mr Lin, in Mandarin, to the whole audience, presumably saying what good work we had all done and, hopefully, complimenting my own, he turned and asked – in halting English – 'Do you like to eat Toy-Toise?'

With this enquiry being reinforced by comments from my interpreter, I soon realised I had not misheard it. I asked him as quietly as possible, 'Does he really mean tortoise?' He said, 'Yes!' I stood there dumbfounded until I managed to come out with, 'It's not something we eat in London.'

Mr Lin, who I knew actually spoke more English than he would admit, heard my statement but ignored it and, in a loud voice, called to the restaurant manager, who stood at the back of the hall. In walked a waiter wearing a white tuxedo uniform, carrying, over his head, a very large blue and white 'willow-patterned' porcelain 'washing-up' bowl. He then proceeded to place this in front of Mr Lin, who told everyone, in simple English, that it contained a sea turtle, or 'Toy-Toise', as he thought I would know it.

He reminded everyone that he knew that I had been in Tianjin many times over the five-year duration of the project.

Then, to my embarrassment, he explained that this meant the project had kept me away for very many months from my family, especially my wife, who he had had the pleasure of meeting in London in 1993 (I said he was a charmer).

He next described that after the turtle was cooked, the two parts of its shell were separated. Sure enough, the waiter lifted up the 'lid' to show everyone this fact. I was looking down at this moment and saw the bottom shell containing all the body meat with four legs sticking out, one in each corner!

Mr Lin invited me to take the top shell, now on a large plate, and eat the membrane that had kept both shell parts together when the turtle was alive. He said this was a famous aphrodisiac and 'very good for the man', so my beautiful wife would enjoy its effect on my return home!

My interpreter whispered that being served this expensive dish and the honour of such a banquet meant I could not refuse this invitation. I began to undertake the challenge of both holding the top shell (its surface was slippery) and eating/swallowing the rubbery membrane attached to its edge. Luckily, I had already been given a Chinese beer, so was able to sip that after each mouthful. I seem to recall this was an interesting combination of tastes. No matter, I was, to much more applause and cheering, eventually able to do justice to the honour I had been given.

**_Not a dish I wish to eat again, nor will I admit if it worked when I was back home!_**

### WHAT! HE'S DRUNK THE MINI BAR DRY – TWICE?

As a young computer engineer, going for the first time to Shanghai in 2008 on business, I decided to take the opportunity to extend my trip to the People's Republic of China by taking some holiday and flying on to Beijing when my IT work was finished. It was recommended to me that I hire a Chinese guide to ensure I made the most of my visit to locations like the capital's Forbidden City and the Great Wall.

This Chinese gentleman was a retired interpreter and translator who had experienced the Cultural Revolution and had no hesitation in telling me about many interesting aspects of his life and, ultimately, the history of the sites we viewed together.

Because the trip was over a couple of days, I had arranged for him to stay in the same hotel as me and our time together was enjoyable. It was also challenging. Firstly, this was because he was a very heavy smoker and secondly, because he tested my friendship when the time came for me to settle our accommodation and refreshment bills as we checked out on the morning of the third day.

The invoice for his room included the complete emptying of the mini bar cabinet on both of the two evenings we had stayed. It was an electronic machine whereby the withdrawal of any of the drinks and food items immediately triggered a signal to the accounts system and the price for each item was loaded irrefutably onto the room bill.

When challenged, as we stood together at the payment desk, he grudgingly admitted that he had certainly enjoyed a whisky before going to bed. I asked how could he have drunk so much else, and eaten so many different chocolate bars and peanuts. He acknowledged that he had been a touch greedy and, opening his travel bag, showed me that he was taking all the unopened items home to his family!

The receptionist said that these 'gifts' could not be credited back to the bill or, for 'health and safety reasons' returned to the hotel, so …

*… I just had to pay the price and not describe it as one of life's learning experiences on my expenses claim.*

## 4)    IS IT ME, OR IS IT THEM?

Have you ever wondered why something happens to you and not others? Have there been times in your life when everything has seemed to be against you and you've felt that you attract misfortune rather than luck?

The following stories demonstrate that sometimes life sends us something unexpected, a 'curve ball'. We just have to do our best at playing it.

That thought may have been in my wife's mind when, whilst standing at the back of our parish church fulfilling her church duties as wedding verger, she heard the mobile phone of one of the wedding guests come to life and speak – in a manly voice – 'I'm sorry but I cannot connect you, please try again later.' Luckily, neither the bride, nor groom, seems to have heard this message. Nor the vicar, as it was actually at the point of the service where he was asking, 'Is there anyone present who knows a reason why these persons may not lawfully marry, to declare it now.'

So, whether it's admitting that a new job may not actually be the one for you, or finding yourself in the wrong location, such occurrences could well lead to you finding more success elsewhere. Whatever your experiences, I do hope you – and Terry Wogan, the British Radio and TV celebrity, who coined the title of this chapter – don't mind being reminded of such occasions, especially if it's anything to do with suggesting you're getting lost due to your partner's misreading of the roadmap …

*Newspaper headings and notices to frighten you …*

POLICE BEGIN CAMPAIGN TO RUN DOWN JAYWALKERS
*What? Think of the paperwork needed to clear up these accidents!*

WAR DIMS HOPE FOR PEACE
*History shows that, unfortunately, it usually does just that.*

IF STRIKE ISN'T SETTLED QUICKLY, IT MAY LAST A WHILE
*(17 weeks, which, speaking personally, was not an enjoyable experience – Ed.)*

LOCAL HIGH SCHOOL DROPOUTS CUT IN HALF
Was this the publicity trailer for the sequel to the Chainsaw Massacre film?

Shop window advert, Cape Town:
ORDER YOUR SUMMER SUIT NOW. BECAUSE OF MUCH BUSINESS
WE EXECUTE CUSTOMERS IN STRICT ROTATION.
*Hopefully, purchasers pay for their clothes when they place their orders.*

In a doctor's surgery, Rome
SPECIALIST IN WOMEN AND OTHER DISEASES

HAVE YOU EVER WONDERED
Why is it that the writing is so small on the complimentary, little bottles
of toiletries, which are provided in the bathrooms of hotels? You only
realise this when you have taken your glasses off, got into the shower,
turned the water on and begun to use body lotion instead of shampoo –
with the resulting lack of bubbles on your head, or in your hair.

## *BEFORE THE AGE OF HAND BAGGAGE RESTRICTIONS*

My meeting finished punctually and I reached Roissy Airport with
time to spare. After checking in, I wandered down to the basement of the
terminal building where there were several, very expensive boutiques,
whose main business appeared to be selling presents for men, with
uneasy consciences, to take home to their wives.

There was also a delicatessen. At one end of its display was a basket
of cheeses that were on their last sell-by dates and, therefore, reasonably
priced. I bought a rather rare one, which I knew would be liked at home,
and placed it in the outer pocket of my small travel case.

After arriving at Heathrow, I took the Piccadilly line on the London
Underground and arrived at Liverpool Street station. Here, as I was
allowed to travel first-class, I found a compartment on a mainline train
that would stop at many stations on its way towards my home in Essex.

With only five occupants, all obviously city types, I settled into the
remaining centre seat of a carriage which, whilst comfortable, I soon
realised was hot and stuffy as this was midsummer. It was not until we
had gone a couple of miles that I realised something was wrong. There
was a very pungent and unpleasant smell coming from my case.

My fellow travellers must have noticed it, too, but I was careful to avoid
eye contact, concentrating instead on reading my newspaper. Strangely,
after only half the journey, I had the compartment to myself, the other
passengers leaving the carriage whether it was their station or not.

Once home, my wife and I began enjoying the cheese, along with a
bottle of red wine. As we did, we wondered if its odour could have been

the reason my fellow travellers vacated the compartment for, whilst the cheese had such a delightful flavour …

*… it smelt like very fresh cow manure!*

## BEWARE A NAKED CLIENT

Early in my career, I did business with a client who I had been warned had a penchant for nudity. This man was known to remove his clothes at random social and business events. Unfortunately, he was way past the age when public nudity is a good idea. (Come to think of it, I don't know if public nudity is ever a good idea at any age.)

At one point in our business relationship, I found it necessary to travel to the southern part of the US to attend a conference with this client. I had a dual purpose for attending, firstly, client relationship building and secondly, I was a guest speaker at the conference. Things went pretty well. The conference was in a great location. The weather was good, warm and sunny. My presentation went well. There were a large number of attendees and they seemed to like what I had to say; it was interactive, I was funny, they liked that, so far so good.

The time I spent with the client and his associates also went very well. His company had a conference hospitality suite (always a good thing for late night partying) and it was to this room that I took a young male colleague who had helped me with the conference presentation. I stayed long enough in the suite to 'grip and grin' with everyone who mattered. I was there to 'see and be seen'. I worked the room and then intended to be on my way, well before any public nudity might occur.

Once I had made my rounds, I was ready to leave. I bid everyone farewell and told my colleague to leave before anyone decided to get naked. I also reminded him we had an early morning flight and we needed to leave for the airport in a few hours' time. We agreed to meet in the hotel lobby at 6.00 am. I left and had a boring time in my hotel room. My colleague stayed, and stayed, and apparently stayed some more, having a great time. So much so, he overslept and we missed our plane!

However, to apologise, he gave me his nice conference plaque that is currently being used as a piece of packing to level the bookcase on my office floor.

By the way, I have not seen my client in the 15 years since and I don't know if my colleague ever did see an undressed part of him on that eventful night.

Perhaps he, or my client, had decided …

### … 'discretion was the better part of valour'!

## FLOWN BEFORE? MOI?

I was travelling in West Africa on a domestic flight and was approached at the aircraft steps on the tarmac by a man who claimed to be in the military. He demanded a cash 'boarding fee' but I refused, and started to walk up the aircraft steps. He grabbed hold of my leg in an attempt to pull me off the aircraft so I kicked out. The last I saw of him he was spread-eagled on the tarmac.

Two days later, I returned to the same airport only to see the same official, by now sporting a black eye, waiting at the bottom of the steps. I borrowed a hat, put on my sunglasses, spoke French and luckily walked away unnoticed.

### Apparently, such extortion attempts were common practice in Africa.

## HAVEN'T I HEARD THIS SOUND SOMEWHERE BEFORE?

I had to go to Paris overnight for an all-day meeting the following day and our travel department duly arranged the flight and the hotel. We were using a proper business travel agent, so when my flight was quite badly delayed, I was comfortable in the knowledge that, in the eventuality I was a late arrival at the hotel, they would have already ensured a room was guaranteed.

Oh how foolish can you be?

For, when I finally arrived at the hotel, I was told that they had no record of my booking. Thankfully, I had the travel agent's confirmation, which forced the receptionist to check further and she triumphantly told me that 'yes,' she had found the reservation but, because I had arrived after 10.00 pm, they had cancelled it and she had no more rooms. Whether the reservation was guaranteed or not was no longer relevant – I needed a room.

The charming and very kind receptionist (but read 'resignedly, doing me a great favour') phoned a sister hotel and confirmed that they could give me a room. She showed me the route on a map, which took me down some characterful side roads at the back of the Place de l'Étoile, a large road junction with the Arc de Triomph at its centre.

After some ten minutes' walk, I arrived, checked in and was taken up four floors in a lift, followed by a final flight of stairs to the only free room, right up in the attic. Ah well, it could have been worse. By now, it was after 11.00 pm so I turned in wondering what was in the large wooden box next to my bed.

I soon found out: every time a guest came back from their night out and took the lift, the box emitted a cacophony of noises as the ancient motor it housed whirred and clanked into action as it dragged the lift upwards. This carried on till sometime after 1.30 am after which exhaustion set in and I dropped off … until about 5.00 am when (I guess) the cook arrived and took the lift to the basement. Then the first guest left, then guests taking early breakfast and so on, with the lift motor springing into action each time I was about to doze off again. Thus, after less than four hours' sleep, I went to my 9.00 am meeting somewhat jaded and fragile.

When the discussion – in French – got into the technicalities of privatisation in a reforming North African country, my mind began to compare the droning of the conversations to the various noises I had enjoyed during the night and, as my concentration wavered, I was not sure I could tell the difference.

**Who says that international consultancy isn't glamorous?**

## HOW NOT TO INFLUENCE THE BOSS

As a young senior manager, I had to attend a European meeting of my peers. This meeting was normally arranged to coincide with an annual European conference. In those heady days, we were allowed to fly business class, but attendees at the conference were told to fly tourist class to save costs. As our meeting was in advance of the conference, we flew business class thinking that we would get away with it.

At the end of the conference, we all duly started our journeys home and boarded our flight back to the UK. I was sitting in business class when several senior partners of the firm walked past, saying hello. Then they realised that they were sitting further down the plane in tourist class! It did not go down well!

The following year, the conference and meeting were set up, but with new rules: everybody to travel tourist, even those travelling in advance – Gotcha!

The conference was duly completed and, once again, the trek home started. Arriving at the airport, we discovered that the flight back to England was delayed due to 'operational difficulties'!

Eventually, another plane was brought into service and passengers were told that names would be announced as seats were allocated. After a few names, mine was called and I duly presented myself to the check-in desk, at which point I was given a boarding pass to a business class seat. How cool, a free upgraded seat, located in the first row of the cabin!

So, boarding-time arrived and I foolishly rushed to get my prized seat. Who should then board but the same senior partners from the year before, on their way to their tourist seats at the rear of the plane. Looking at me in total disbelief, they once again passed me by, shaking their heads in dismay without saying a word.

*A few days later, I was asked to explain how I had wangled an upgrade. I just gave an enigmatic smile and moved the conversation on. (I never did find out why!)*

## I REQUESTED A LONG WEIGHT. RECEIVED A LONG WAIT!

At the start of my student engineering apprenticeship, I was introduced to the concept of a 'long wait'. This wasn't some piece of manufacturing equipment, rather a trick to introduce me, a young and innocent ex-schoolboy, to the real world. As an apprentice, you were managed by a chargehand and, in this case, he sent me to collect, using a stores ticket, something called 'A Long Weight'. On arrival at the main hatch of the central stores, I was told to 'hang-on' whilst the storeman went away to find it.

After quite some time (I think you can see where this is going) I began to get anxious that nothing was being provided and, being a 'new boy' in my first week, was keen to get back to my workbench. However, before that happened, I was then sent around the corner to the second hatch and, once again, told to 'hang on' while they hunted for this elusive piece of equipment. Time sped past and in the end, and in frustration, I said I would go back to report that they didn't seem to have one of these items in stock.

On returning to the workshop, the chargehand told me to go to see his boss, the foreman. This person was the equivalent of God to an apprentice. He occupied a central office that everyone could see and, of course, he was soon on display questioning me as to why I had been away from my bench so long. Whilst I gave my explanation he interrupted to say, 'Welcome to the world of work' and let me off with a smile. As I left the

Chip monk

office, a big cheer from all the other workers went up as the chargehand had sent the word around that another young apprentice had been inducted into the world of factory fun.

**_Needless to say, I later thanked the storemen for being so helpful._**

## IF YOU ARE NOT WITH ME – THEN YOU REALLY ARE NOT WITH ME!

When I entered my first management role, I had a very kind boss who did whatever he could to help me be a success. However, there were times when I wished he hadn't helped.

Prior to personal computers, many people were employed as typists and almost every office/department had at least one. My own office was no different, and we had three in a department of ten staff. I had never recruited before, so before my boss went away on an extended business trip, he quickly employed a German lady, who would type and operate the Telex machine and stand in for one of the regular typists who was going to be away on holiday at the same time.

On her first day, Helga was late and then she was late every day of her first week by at least an hour. I spoke to her about this and was told she wasn't late; she was here on time every day.

This somewhat puzzled me, so I told her exactly what time she had arrived every day of that first week. 'Ah,' said Helga, 'I wasn't here physically, however, at 9.00 am every morning I was here mentally.' I had to inform her it was her physical presence that was required but all I got was a blank look. She obviously wasn't with me mentally.

During her first week, her output was incredibly low, even taking into account her lateness, and I asked her to explain why. She said that, in spite of it being a company based in England, she could only work on a German keyboard.

**_At this point, I informed her I had to let her go, as her presence was no longer required, physically, mentally, with or without a keyboard!_**

## NEXT TIME, PLEASE SAY WHAT YOU MEAN!

A few years ago, I attended a week-long workshop in Siberia. As usual, at these annual workshops that took place across the former Soviet Union, the session on the last day (Thursday) would end at lunchtime to be followed by an afternoon and an evening of drinking and eating by the delegates. This particular workshop was no different and the 50 or so people involved enjoyed a good 'session'.

We were all due to be picked up by bus the next morning, at 6.00 am, to make the hour-long journey to the airport for the long flight to Moscow to connect with the flight back to London. However, many of the participants decided that, rather than having a couple of hours of sleep, they would continue drinking until the bus arrived – as a total of 18 hours solid drinking was then possible!

On arrival at the airport, the bus dropped us all off with our luggage and then departed, leaving very many of the group (including me) nursing their hangovers and all looking sorry for themselves.

At check-in, we were told our Aeroflot flight had not left Moscow and that we would be delayed by at least seven hours. One of our office staff phoned Moscow to arrange for a bus to come to pick us all up and take us to a hotel where we could get some food and rest. A bus duly arrived, the driver got out, locked the bus and left. We had asked for a bus, but no one had thought of asking for a driver, too.

After a second call to Moscow to explain our predicament, a driver turned up – but as we had not made the proper request – without keys for the bus! Therefore, we now had a bus, a driver, but no keys, and many very hung-over British and Russian delegates probably forgetting much of what they had learnt on the workshop.

A third call to Moscow resulted in the arrival of another driver, but he, too, had no keys! So, we gave up and collapsed on the pavement to wait for what seemed like hours until Aeroflot finally sent our plane and we boarded, very much the worse for wear.

That should have been the end of the saga, but Russia had not finished giving us excitement. (Or stress at least.) Upon arrival in Moscow, a smiling check-in clerk said our plane to London had left and we had to buy new tickets. After hearing our saga of the buses, and admitting that the Aeroflot plane had failed to turn up on time, she added insult to injury, by saying – in strong 'Russian-English' – that …

***… we had caused our own problems by not being clear we needed a bus with a driver and keys the first time!***

Postscript: If I ever return to any part of Russia, and need my own transport, I will ensure I ask for a bus with seats, tyres, wheels, etc, etc!

## PERHAPS CRIME DOES PAY?

We recently broke up a mugging attempt outside our office door in downtown St Paul, Minnesota, North America. The mugger ran off, the victim was fine, her purse and mobile phone were intact and we all, more or less, made the decision to let the guy go, not knowing what we would have done had we caught him.

Later, we learnt from the local TV news that one of the people who helped us break up the robbery attempt had since been arrested, charged with churning his client's financial accounts and defrauding the company.

**Perhaps the mugger's motive was to get some cash for this person?**

## PERHAPS I WASN'T MEANT TO WORK THERE ANYWAY!

I am nearing Harrogate in North Yorkshire, in a rush for an important appointment. Running short of time and diesel, and getting more flustered by the moment, I pull into a motorway service station.

With a queue of cars at the diesel pumps, I decide to use the equipment designated for lorries and trucks, only to find that the nozzle on the filling pipe is too big to fit into the spout of my car's tank and the pressure the diesel is being delivered at is many times what I'm familiar with.

Result – half the delivered fuel is over the side of the car. The other half is down my trousers, over my shoes and spreading over the forecourt.

Now desperate and embarrassed in equal measure, I seek refuge in the cloakroom to clean myself up as well as I can. Despite my best efforts, I look and smell interesting to say the least, but arrive just at the agreed time for the meeting.

As I say, this all happened before a meeting, which was actually a job interview. This was then conducted in a haze of diesel fumes. The interviewer said nothing about my appearance and 'aroma' but …

**… I wondered later if these aspects were the reasons I did not get the job.**

## PUTTING MY BEST FEET FORWARD FOR A JOB INTERVIEW

I had been invited to attend a job interview for a senior position and decided to take my wife with me and show her the area where we might be living. The location was several hours drive away, and it was high summer.

I decided to put my best suit on a hanger behind our small car's front seats and change somewhere close to the large office I was to visit.

All went well until the time to get ready, in a nearby lay-by, at which point we realised I had left my shoes at home. I knew the organisation I was visiting was rather old-fashioned, so we did not think sandals were really the things to wear with a business suit.

As I began to panic about spoiling my chances of gaining employment, my wife had the brainwave of suggesting we drive to the nearby town and see if it had a Marks & Spencer's department store. It did and, at this time, you were allowed to drive right to the store's door and stop at the kerb. We did and I dashed in to purchase some appropriate footwear.

Returning to the pavement, I saw my wife driving towards me having just completed a circuit of the high street and, with minutes to spare, she chauffeured me to the interview. Once inside the offices, and then touring the organisation's extensive production area, I wondered if I was appearing fragile as I was trying to tread very carefully to avoid scuffing or marking these new shoes.

The reason for this was that, as I already owned several similar pairs of shoes and money was tight (I was in between jobs), I didn't need any more footwear. So, following the interview, we repeated the trip to the store, returned the shoes as if 'not worn' – just the wrong selection – and quickly left the town.

My embarrassment on completing this action was compounded by the fact that I wasn't offered the job.

**Perhaps they wanted someone who was going to be much firmer when 'walking the job'?**

## WAS IT A MISTAKE, SHOULD WE HAVE BEEN NEXT DOOR?

In my early twenties, I was the new PA to the UK Chief Executive of a major French company and, to my delight, I was invited, together with the Operations Director and his wife, to accompany him to an international conference in Paris.

My boss was a rather enigmatic character whom I hadn't yet got to know very well, apart from the fact that he loved jazz, seemed a bon vivant gentleman and was keen that we should all make the most of the trip. On the eve of the conference, he announced that he was going to take us out to one of his favourite clubs.

Our taxi took us to a narrow street just off the Champs-Elysées and we followed him down some dimly-lit steps into a basement, where we were greeted enthusiastically and seated in the front row of velvet-covered chairs next to the stage.

What followed may have been no surprise to some, but I had never been to a strip club before, let alone witnessed some of the 'gymnastics' performed in front of us! As the only fluent French speaker, I was somewhat aghast when the Irish wife of the Operations Director was then called upon by the compère to go up on stage and sing ribald songs to the great amusement of the rest of the audience. She clearly had no idea what she was singing, but the champagne helped loosen her vocal chords and we all had a good time, however puzzling I had found the choice of venue.

*Years later, when I discovered that one of the most famous jazz clubs in Paris happened to be next door to a certain strip club, I wondered if the Chief Executive really loved music as much as he made out – or girls even more.*

## WHICH GIRL, OR GIRLS, YOU LIKE TO ENJOY?

On behalf of the World Bank, I was going to meet the executives of a major battery manufacturer in the Guangzhou province of China. This is a tax-free enterprise zone just over the border with Hong Kong.

It's that word – enterprise – I now want to focus on.

As a result of a misunderstanding, the most senior executive was not available to host part of my visit and so the rest of the visit was cancelled. Such was his embarrassment, because of the considerable effort in arranging my meeting and the special flight involved, that he offered, as compensation, 'a night on the town'!

This involved being collected by a junior staff member from my local hotel and taken, by him as my host, to a Chinese nightclub, located in one of the plushest hotels 'downtown'. First, there was dinner in a smart restaurant, then afterwards liqueurs and an invitation to move to another part of the building.

We went through what seemed to be a side door and entered a very large foyer, with sweeping staircase in the style of a horseshoe.

I particularly noticed this because on about every fifth stair, as I ascended, there stood a very attractive young lady hostess wearing a figure-hugging evening dress of the sort that left nothing much to the imagination, in one of six different colours.

(This spectacle was replicated on the stairs on the other side.)

Each young lady smiled as we walked up the staircase. From the landing at the top, we walked down a long corridor, on each side of which were obviously individual karaoke rooms. If you're not familiar with the Chinese office worker's habit of having a singsong in front of the dancing ball of the karaoke TV, after work, then let me say I don't think you've missed much.

Going through the double doors at the end of the corridor, we were suddenly in a very large dance floor area with a stage. I would imagine we were over the restaurant I'd been in earlier.

In front of the stage was a series of Chesterfield sofas, on each side of which were individual leather chairs. In other words, if you sat on the sofa you were trapped by whoever was in the chairs!

This was definitely the technique that I was exposed to, for no sooner had we sat down, than a slightly older hostess appeared, introduced herself and sat down with us.

The company executive made it clear that this person was going to be 'in charge of us' for the evening. He began to enjoy a conversation with her in Mandarin, with an occasional English comment to me. At one point, he asked if I would like anything to drink.

Before answering, I took time to look around the whole area and noticed that I was the only guest, a glass of champagne was already arriving courtesy of yet another hostess and the young ladies, who had been standing on the staircase, were now gathering in a darkened area behind me.

I didn't have time to pay that much more attention, as suddenly the stage was lit up and a group of young 'exotic' dancers began their show time routine. Whilst their costumes were all very colourful, and they certainly looked very attractive, their dancing was never completely synchronised. Consequently, I had great difficulty not laughing about the fact that the arm movements of the dancers at the back always seemed to be a few seconds later than those of the dancers at the front.

However, I found it quite surprising when the executive explained that this whole routine and ensemble had been commissioned for my sole entertainment – as a very sincere apology from the company to someone from such an important organisation.

When I had a chance, I asked the 'the lady in charge of us' why all the young ladies from the staircase had arrived behind me, why those girls in the matching coloured evening dresses were now in pairs, and what that meant.

With much smiling from her, and indeed the company's junior staff member, she replied that I could choose a young woman (or women) based on what colour I liked. She would then tell me what their particular speciality was!

It seemed that this was intended to be a very generous way of the company saying sorry for embarrassing me with a wasted trip to their factory.

I explained I had another series of meetings the next day and so could not stay any longer, as I needed to be up early. Therefore, I must refuse the kind offer …

They were both shocked at my announcement but I stressed the gesture was nevertheless appreciated as I got up to walk towards the door and the exit corridor, whilst the young Chinese businessman remained seated.

*I didn't get to meet him the next morning. However, as I checked out, the receptionist gave me his apologies saying, 'He was tied up.' Perhaps he is still there trying weakly to escape those enterprising ladies?*

## 5)    *GETTING THERE AND, HOPEFULLY, GETTING BACK*

This chapter is mainly about the trials and tribulations of air travel, as exemplified by the 'Happy landings with Roger' story. We take for granted the operational smoothness of international airports, the huge range of flights, their implicit safety, the skill and experience of the pilots, the 'ease' of getting through the x-ray and security stations and the expectation that our luggage will arrive at the same time as we do. These are all conditions that underpin successful travel, whether for business or pleasure.

Therefore, apologies if the stories that follow alarm you. They say that air travel is the safest form of getting from A to B. In the 1990s, a study by Boeing showed that flying in a commercial airliner was 20 times safer than travelling by car. But, hey, don't they build planes not cars – so they would say that wouldn't they?

Seeing a wheel of the plane you're sitting in roll past the cabin window or experiencing a possible missile attack are not situations any of us would enjoy, whatever type of trip we're on. However, with an average of 26,000 flights a day across Europe, it's a relief that such incidents are not more common.

*Newspaper headings and notices to get you anxious …*

JUVENILE COURT TO TRY SHOOTING DEFENDANTS
*See if that works any better than a fair trial or as a deterrent to other young people.*

MAN STRUCK BY LIGHTNING: FACES BATTERY CHARGE
*He probably is the battery charger!*

ASTRONAUT TAKES BLAME FOR GAS IN SPACECRAFT
*That's what he gets for eating baked beans three times a day!*

On the room card in a hotel in Kuala Lumpur:
YOU ARE KINDLY INVITED TO TAKE ADVANTAGE OF THE CHAMBERMAID

On a one way road to the Victoria Falls in Zimbabwe:
TAKE NOTIE: WHEN THIS SIGN IS UNDERWATER, THIS ROAD IS IMPASSABLE
(The turning circle was at the end of the road and by the time you had reached it you would have been wet through or worse!)

A sign in the window of a dentist in The Rocks area of Sydney:
TEETH ARE EXTRACTED BY THE MOST MODERN METHODIST

HAVEN'T WE BEEN HERE BEFORE?
Why is it that the return trip from anywhere new is always a lot shorter,
and quicker, than when you travelled to it?

## A DIFFERENT KIND OF POLITICAL CLEAN SWEEP

*The following is an extract from Last Man Standing: Memoirs of a Political Survivor by the*
*Rt Hon Jack Straw MP, former Home Secretary, Foreign Secretary and Leader of the House of*
*Commons during Tony Blair's premiership, and Secretary of State for Justice and Lord Chancellor*
*under Gordon Brown. It is reproduced with kind permission of Macmillan; London, 2012,*
*p 343-344.*

I made my first visit of many to Afghanistan in mid-February 2002,
travelling there via meetings in Turkey, Israel and the Occupied Territories.
I had invited both Michael Ancram (now Lord Lothian), the Shadow
Foreign Secretary, and the Liberal Democrats' foreign affairs spokesman,
Ming Campbell. Michael could not come, but Ming joined me for the trip.

The last leg of the journey to Kabul, in the dead of night, was in an RAF
Hercules transport plane. We all had to don the heavy bulletproof jackets
and helmets with which I was to become very familiar. The passengers
sat on webbing seats. The loo was a bucket. Because there were women
on the flight, the RAF had rigged a sheet of plastic around it for modesty;
usually they didn't bother.

I was invited to sit in the cockpit. This was one of the older 'Hercs',
with a four-man crew – two pilots, an engineer and a navigator. Once
over Afghan airspace, two other crew – 'loadmasters' – came up from the
back of the plane and began to scour the skies with night-vision goggles,
looking for any signs of ground-to-air rockets that might impede our
journey. The US had given the Pakistanis at least 2,000 Stinger missiles
for use by the Mujahedeen against the Soviets, and there was no way of
knowing whether some of these were still available to the Taliban.

We'd had the news that most of the runway lights at Kabul Airport
had been knocked out by an earlier plane; and that President Karzai's
civil aviation and tourism minister, Abdul Rahman, had that day been
assassinated by a mob of hajjis – pilgrims – at the airport, angry that they
had been kept waiting for a plane to Mecca. There was therefore a little
nervousness as we came in for final approach. 'One hundred feet, eighty,
sixty, fifty, forty,' went the navigator. 'F*** and s***; what the hell is that?'
cut in the pilot, swerving as we touched down.

The pilot, with good reason, thought that a man he had spotted in the middle of the runway had a rifle in his hand. It was in fact a broom. The man had been sent out to sweep the runway, and simply hadn't noticed our arrival.

**_Fortunately, he was safe, and so were we._**

## A TRIP TO REMEMBER – OR PERHAPS FORGET?

It was early summer 1974, Christine (my wife) and I, with two friends, John and Kate, were going for a holiday in an apartment in Catalonia. With four drivers amongst us, we decided to drive there, hopefully, within 24 hours.

We packed our cases into the boot and onto the roof rack of our Triumph 1300 saloon car parked on our sloping driveway. Ready to go, we carefully reversed, fully loaded with luggage and the four of us, out onto the main road. As we did so, we heard a slight scraping noise but did not take any notice at the time.

We caught a ferry from Dover at 10.00 pm and landed at Calais around midnight. All went well as we drove into the moonlit French countryside but, as dawn broke and the outside temperature increased, the car decided to overheat. We stopped at a service station near Lyons to buy fuel and top up the radiator. However, there was a queue for the pumps and, while we waited, the car stalled and would not restart. The staff from the filling station ran out and we thought, 'Oh good, they are going to help.' This was not to be, as, with much shouting, they simply pushed the car to one side so the petrol queue could make progress. After waiting 20 minutes to let the car cool down, we topped up the radiator with water from a thoughtfully provided watering can and set off again.

We had only been going about an hour when the car decided to overheat once more. An emergency stop on the hard shoulder of the French motorway quickly followed. On the other side of the fence, we noticed a pond so John bravely climbed over to fill a container with water. Just then, a police car, plus a police van, both with blue flashing lights, screeched to a halt alongside our parked car. We thought we were going to be arrested! Fortunately, Christine spoke excellent French and was able to explain to the many gendarmes what had happened. They were all facing the motorway and one advised that we should wait 20 minutes and then restart our journey.

Luckily, they all failed to notice John climbing back over the fence, with the filled container and wet feet. It was not until they had driven off into the distance that we used the water and waited the required time, and some more to be sure.

Unfortunately, as we travelled further into Southern France and then Spain, the car continued to boil frequently. Eventually, John, having some car-maintenance knowledge, removed the thermostat and made an emergency repair with some double-sided masking tape that we just happened to have in the boot. This excellent improvisation enabled us to make steady progress and we finally reached our destination in the early evening.

However, by the time we arrived at our apartment, the car was making a loud roaring noise. Looking underneath the boot of the car, all four of us realised we had suffered all the various excitements (and challenging moments) on our way through France to Spain, because we had damaged the exhaust pipe and silencer when reversing out of our driveway!

We had an excellent holiday, made even better once a local garage was able to repair our car by replacing the silencer with one made for another make of car.

**The Spanish mechanic's use of his hammer, to effect the improvisation of joining two dissimilar exhaust tubes together, was an impressive sight.**

In planning the time of our return, we all agreed we should not push our temporary exhaust pipe too much and instead have a more leisurely journey home, driving overnight and sleeping during the two allocated days.

Arriving back in Dover late in the afternoon of the third day, we decided to have a final meal together. We chose a smart looking steak house belonging to Raab Inns. After all the fine food in Spain and France, it was the worst thing we could have done! Two of us ordered half a roast duck each. However, when the obviously shared duck was served all we could see was a very large layer of inedible fat. We felt sure the dish had not long been liberated from the nearby village duck pond!

About two weeks after our visit, we read that the restaurant was destroyed in a major fire. We thought that a fitting revenge for our meal but I would like to report …

**… we had nothing to do with its destruction!**

## *DID YOU SEE WHAT I JUST SAW?*

My parents and my younger sister were on a flight to Croatia for their annual holiday at a time when such flights were just beginning after the fall of the Berlin wall. As they landed and were travelling at some speed down the runway, the gentleman sitting next to my father turned to him and calmly said, 'Did you see what I just saw out of the window, or was I imagining it?'

My father replied just as calmly, 'Yes, I did see a wheel rolling alongside us.'

Apparently, it was one off the plane they were all sitting in. The plane stopped safely but, in doing so, caused quite a commotion, including the arrival of several fire engines with their lights flashing and sirens blaring, and the hasty evacuation of all the passengers.

*Needless to say, my relatives made sure that all the wheels were bolted firmly onto the plane for the flight home!*

## *DON'T WORRY, THE DUMMY FROM AIRPLANE! IS FLYING US BACK TO THE UK*

In 2000 I'd finished doing business in St Paul's, the capital of the American state of Minnesota, so began my return journey to the UK by taking an internal American Airlines flight to Washington, as I had a connecting ticket from Dulles Airport back to Heathrow.

Experiencing severe headwinds, going east across the US, the plane from St Paul's was late arriving at the extensive terminal. This meant I did not have enough time to get to the appropriate gate, in one of the transfer areas, to catch my flight home to London, not even by using the Aerotrain that travels around the four concourse areas.

Explaining my predicament to one of the airline staff, I was soon on an electric 'courtesy cart' with its light flashing and being rushed through the passenger halls, as it was quite some way to get to the check-in area for the 8.00 pm flight to London.

Little did I know that they needn't have bothered, although the gesture was appreciated. For taking off on time and then arriving on time were not going to be characteristics of the forthcoming flight.

After boarding in the usual way and taking our seats, I'm sure all of us began to wonder why the plane was still sitting on the runway, well after departure time. We were eventually told that the cargo loading team could not get its freight hatch door locked – there were problems making the rubber seal around it airtight – so we had to stay in our seats while they continued to run the engines to test for leaks. Without the seal working properly, we could not take-off!

I don't remember this technical explanation doing much to reassure us for the forthcoming flight.

Eventually, at about 10.30 pm, we were asked to disembark and make our way to a reception area, which, in fact, became a 'limbo-land' as we were neither in America nor the UK, having boarded a flight, then been asked to leave it to go to an area with no customs control. Again, this was not reassuring, especially when all of us from a full 747 found we were in an area with just a few toilets and only one vending machine that soon ran out of cans of drink.

After about 40 minutes, we were told to re-board, take our seats quickly and get ready for a take-off planned at midnight.

Such excitement was unnecessary; as no sooner had we started taxiing down the runway than the plane suddenly stopped. Another announcement told us that we had just hit a deer! Then another, that we must wait for an inspection crew to drive out and look at the undercarriage and landing wheels to see if they were damaged. (I don't think they really thought they were, given we were in a jumbo jet and this was just a small animal that we'd run over, but …)

After watching the inspection crew vehicle drive around with its lights flashing and people pointing at our plane's undercarriage, we took off at 30 minutes after midnight, only four and half hours later than our scheduled departure time.

*A key point to note for later is the fact that during all this time our engines had been running and so burning fuel.*

The in-flight meal was quickly served, the lights were turned down and those of us still awake began to watch the film being shown on the overhead screens. Others of us continued to talk to passengers around us. I did that with my neighbour, Hank, a big Texan American football quarterback. I told him that soccer was real football and we hit it off and began to talk quietly as neither of us felt tired. The cabin crew weren't either as they certainly kept us business class travellers supplied with drinks and nibbles.

I'm not sure when, but say at about 3.00 am, the pilot – we knew that because of his very smart uniform and the four rings on the arms of his jacket – came walking towards us, then sat on the arm of a nearby seat and said he wanted to personally apologise for the problems of take-off and the delay that had occurred.

He hoped he would be able to make up the lost time but he then asked if we had felt the turbulence caused by the strong headwinds that we were flying into, which would certainly slow us down.

Before thinking about discussing the weather, I took a close look at him and asked if he realised he looked very much like Peter Graves, the comedy actor who played the pilot in the 1980s Hollywood film 'Airplane!' and, if indeed he was him, was the plane flying on 'automatic pilot'?

He replied in a quiet voice that yes, he was often mistaken for the film's Captain Clarence Oveur, yes, the plane was on automatic control and yes, the blow-up dummy, as in the film, was in the pilot seat – 'but please don't tell everybody, I don't wish to start a panic.'

Hank and I laughed, appreciating this unusual frankness and good humour. We also learnt that this was because it was the pilot's last flight to the UK. He was then retiring and flying back as a passenger after a holiday, so he was in quite a 'demob-happy' mood.

Unfortunately, the three of us did not realise that the American woman sitting next to me was actually awake, rather than, as we'd assumed, asleep under a blanket. She stirred and proceeded to tell us that the conversation was not funny, and that she would be reporting the flight and the captain when we landed.

Little did she know that she would have some additional things to report in a couple of hours' time.

The pilot left and Hank and I decided to try and sleep, but it would certainly be a struggle as by then the headwind turbulence was building and we were strapped in and, as they say in the States, 'hunkered down'.

As the dawn sunlight woke me (a cabin window nearby did not have its blind down), I believed we were somewhere over the approaches to the Irish coast. However, we were suddenly told we were quite a bit nearer to dry land. In fact, our friend the pilot announced we were soon going to make an emergency landing on the coast of England as we were running out of fuel!

The woman next to me started swearing in a shocked and frightened manner. Hank and I, on the other hand, started discussing what might have caused this situation. We agreed that the problem was the engines being kept running whilst they tested the air pressure of the freight hatch and, of course, the extra delay as the wheels were checked for 'deer damage'. These possible reasons were endorsed by another announcement explaining just such facts.

## Congratulations on passing your test!
### Now you can learn the real meaning of Highway code!

**Roundabouts**; when the music stops be careful of people getting off.

**Towing**; it can be very painful having a vehicle on toe.

**Vision**; for good vision try the road to Damascus.

**The horn** should not be played when driving but a trombon can be played in a convertible.

Inform the **Highways Agency** if you see a broken white lin

When you see **double white lines** you've had enough vodka.

Areas of white painted stripes are to be entered when you want a head on collision.

**Mini roundabouts** are usually encountered when driving across playgrounds.

**Reversing**; always reverse backwards.

## Now you have passed your test
### you can learn the "real" Highway Code!

If you see a **zebra** or a **pelican crossing**, sober up.

A **toucan crossing** is for lager drinkers.

A **puffin crossing** does not denote a steam railway.

If you see **horse riders** give them some lozenges.

**ial carriageways**; beware of people brandishing swords pistols.

**is lanes** may be used by cars when carrying more than 16 ssengers

93

As we prepared to reach safety, before all the fuel ran out, I realised we were going to land at Cardiff Airport, which had, in fact, been a World War II landing strip built to take B-52 bombers, so there was plenty of runway for us to use in an equivalent sized 747.

Touchdown was smooth and visibility clear, but the woman next to me could only see fields rather than the reassuring sight of a stretch of concrete like on a normal airfield. Accordingly, she became very agitated, especially by the sight of cows grazing on grass that to her seemed very close-by. Of course, the height of our plane and the way we had landed gave the impression that we were running down a grass track and likely to slip off towards the seashore, which we could see ran quite close to this airport.

*Not good for her nerves and another potential point in her forthcoming complaint.*

Hank on the other hand, looking out of another window, saw only a series of terminal buildings. These had the appearance of being several rows of double height shipping containers. On top of these was a very impressive sign that said, in Welsh 'Croeso i Gymru a Maes Awyr Rhyngwladol Caerdydd' and underneath in English 'Welcome to Wales and Cardiff International Airport.'

Hank asked with some concern, and in a broad Texan voice, 'Where is this Way-less, it's not a country I've heard of?'

At this point, my neighbour was also asking similar questions mainly to herself, but in earshot of us both. (Unfortunately, I got the distinct impression that neither of them knew much about 'what was on the British side of the pond'.)

Before I could develop a geography lesson, our friend the pilot made another exciting announcement. He informed us that he had organised the refuelling of the plane and we didn't have to worry about paying for the extra fuel – he'd got the company credit card!

After this message, 'you know who' was really steaming and her language extremely expressive. Hank and I thought it was a great gesture on the pilot's part as we laughed and shared the fact that neither of us could have helped, as we did not have much cash in our pockets.

*By the way, I meant to tell you that this plane should have landed at Heathrow at six in the morning. The refuelling was taking place at about 9.00 am. So, during the night, we had made up about 90 minutes of the four and half hours lost before we took off, in spite of having a very bumpy flight.*

At 10.00 am sharp, we took off for our destination having been assured, again by our friend upfront, that we would be landing in one hour's time.

It wasn't far to fly over England to our destination.

Can I suggest you know what's coming next? We hadn't got far, probably just over the Bristol Channel, which I could see below, when we were told, 'Sorry, you know that slot we had booked at Heathrow, well we've lost it. However, what this does mean is that I can do a circuit around London and show all you first-time visitors the whole great city.'

*I don't think the last comment really helped my neighbour's blood pressure.*

The pilot did as he promised, showing us the sights, including the Houses of Parliament, Tower Bridge and Buckingham Palace and kindly banking the plane at the appropriate places, so everyone had a good view.

Eventually, at 12 noon to the minute, we touched down at Heathrow to a great cheer from all on board – except by 'you know who'. She kept silent.

As Hank and I made our goodbyes to each other, and shook the hand of the pilot who stood at the door of the flight deck without his jacket, we warned him of the imminent arrival of the very irate passenger who had sat next to me. He thanked us, and then said in a loud voice:

**'I've now officially retired on full pay and am just like both of you, an ordinary passenger on this plane – I don't know where the pilot, automatic or real, has gone!'**

Postscript: Airplane! is one of the most enjoyable comedy films about flying ever made! This spoof disaster movie stars Robert Hayes as a passenger called on to fly a plane after its pilots are taken ill mid-flight. More importantly, it features Leslie Nielsen (who would later perform a glorious role in the Naked Gun films) as a deliciously deadpan doctor. His answer to the question 'Surely there must be something you can do?', 'I'm doing everything I can – and stop calling me Shirley' has entered film history. I invite readers to view the Dummy scene in the You Tube or Google clip: Airplane! (2/10) Movie CLIP - Automatic Pilot (1980) HD

*As you have just read about a pilot, here is the first of another three anecdotes that describe those brave men and women of the skies.*

## HAPPY LANDINGS WITH ROGER

*The following is an extract from an article by the journalist Alison Pearson on Thursday, 2 February 2012. It is reproduced with kind permission of the Daily Telegraph newspaper.*

When I get on a plane, I don't know how the flight is going to go until I hear the pilot speak. What I want to hear is Roger from Weybridge. You know Roger – RAF, Dambusters raid, home from a mission, quick shower and shave, then out with Kay Kendall in the Morgan. Terrific handling. That's the car and not the actress. Roger is not only blessed with nerves of steel in a crisis, he has a voice that is three parts Cognac to two parts walnut dashboard. If I hear darling Roger when I get on board, I am fine.

I may be a pilot snob, but clearly I am not alone. The traditional well-spoken pilot's voice in a clipped Home Counties accent has been voted the best of all in a survey of regular travellers.

Cockney came out worst, followed by the Midlands accent. I most definitely do not want a pilot like the one on a night flight to Jordan, who said, 'Call me Mike,' before announcing that he could not switch the lights off on my side of the aisle, 'Because I'm worried all the electrics will cut out if I do!'

**The moral is, don't be flown by anyone who sounds like a DJ. Fly Roger.**

## I'D RATHER HE'D SPENT HIS TIME DIFFERENTLY!

I hesitate to recall the memorable trip to Moldova when the country was part of the Soviet Union. We took off from Frankfurt (as the UK Civil Aviation Authority would not allow Air Moldova anywhere near our skies due to issues about the safety of their planes) and I was sitting at the front of an ancient Russian Yak plane.

No sooner had we reached a cruising altitude than the pilot came out of the cockpit, sat down next to me, had three shots of vodka from a hip flask and then went to sleep for the whole journey …

**… only waking up 15 minutes before landing!**

## JUST ANOTHER DAY IN THE CZECH REPUBLIC

Shortly after the Berlin Wall came down and the breakup of the former Soviet Bloc, I was invited to visit an electronics engineering company in the newly formed Czech Republic. This country was keen to set up a number of industry-based joint ventures with European organisations.

The company was based some distance from Prague and, whilst it was possible to fly to Prague, I did not look forward to the long drive of several hours to the company's location. I decided it would be far easier to take the HS125 company jet, but soon discovered that I had to get permission from the chief of the Czech Air Force to fly anywhere else other than Prague.

We contacted the chief who eventually gave us permission, but only on the basis that we had one of his navigators to guide us there. We, of course, were not allowed to see the maps or the information they contained. Still, I thought, better that than the long, tedious road journey.

I flew to Prague the night before and met our appointed co-pilot in the hotel lobby the next morning. Alarmingly, he was wearing a neck brace!!! Apparently, he had ejected from his fighter plane and had injured himself, but was still deemed fit enough to take the role of a navigator!

We took off from Prague with the navigator sitting up front with the pilot. The weather was dreadful, raining and there was a very low cloud base of a few hundred feet. The flight took about 45 minutes and, still in the cloud base, we started to descend, preparing to land.

As we dropped out of the cloud base into the heavy rain, probably at a height of a few hundred feet, my lasting memory is hearing my pilot shout 'Where's the runway?'

Seconds later, he put the engines to full power and we disappeared back up into the clouds. Air Traffic Control and our navigator had brought us down parallel to the runway but 300 metres to one side. The next approach was better and we eventually landed. We were the first Western aircraft to land at what had been a former Soviet bomber station.

The irony of this tale is that one of the products made by the company I visited was air traffic control radars.

**We certainly could have done with a better radar system (or navigator) that day.**

## NOT A DISASTER MOVIE – JUST MY TRIP

On a business trip to the US, a colleague and I had spent some time in the San Francisco Bay area, visiting various companies. The next destination was Rolling Meadows, near Chicago, and together we caught a midday flight out of San Francisco.

Arriving at the hotel in Rolling Meadows (no sign of any meadows by the way), I switched on the TV in my bedroom in order to catch up with the news before going out for dinner. I was horrified to see a trail of destruction in San Francisco following a major 6.9 magnitude earthquake, which had occurred shortly after our plane had taken off.

We finished our business in Rolling Meadows and flew out of O'Hare to the next stop, New York.

Once there, I again settled into a hotel, switched on the TV and saw that a car driver at O'Hare had ploughed into the crowd at the terminal building, resulting in several fatalities. We had been at the very same spot a few hours before it happened!

Departure from New York had a few of our American colleagues keeping a nervous eye on the news but, fortunately, we got away safely with no incidents this time.

**As they say in Las Vegas, Lady Luck was with me all the way.**

## ROUTINE FLIGHTS? DON'T THINK THESE TWO WERE

### Please beam me up Scottie

Over the years, I have often flown for business on 'day-trips' to Guernsey. On this particular occasion, it was to meet a client from Yorkshire who flew to Guernsey from East Midlands Airport, while I flew from Gatwick.

Both of us arrived on the morning's first flights, worked hard and unexpectedly finished our business early. At noon, we decided to return directly to the airport for our flights at around 3.00 pm, as the weather was too dull for sightseeing.

We arrived at the terminal to find the East Midlands flight was scheduled before my Gatwick flight. As we sat in the lounge, catching up on messages on our mobile phones, I happened to look up and realised that all the planes I had seen standing outside, only minutes earlier, had now disappeared. Fog had drifted in and was obscuring visibility!

I turned to my colleague (who was involved in an argument on the phone) nudged him, and pointed out of the window. His face was a picture of shock and he quickly ended his call. We discussed the implications of this weather on our busy diaries.

In due course, over the Tannoy, came the news that an inbound flight from Southampton was circling somewhere in the clouds above. Then, that my Gatwick flight was overhead and, finally, that my client's East Midlands plane was also approaching.

'Thank goodness for radar,' we each said as we discussed our chances of reaching home that night. We also wondered if the hotel we had just vacated would have rooms for us if we were marooned.

Our fears of staying overnight were heightened when it was announced that the Southampton flight was returning to base.

However, after what seemed like an eternity (but was probably only ten minutes), we were told the Gatwick flight was preparing to land, quickly followed by the same news for the East Midlands flight. All of us in the departure lounge held our breath in the hope that the landings were successful, and they were.

After that stressful time, we then waited anxiously for the announcement that our flights were ready for take-off as the fog was still swirling. It seemed doubtful that our incarceration on Guernsey would shortly be ended or that we would return to the UK that day.

Eventually, my client's East Midlands flight took off – but into the fog – on its way to Jersey.

When, later, my Gatwick flight was called, the fog had lifted and I enjoyed an uneventful flight to Gatwick.

However, on entering the arrivals concourse, before immigration control, everyone from my flight joined a very large crowd of international passengers. Finding an official, some of us explained we had been on an internal flight, so did not need to be 'controlled'. Luckily, he kindly led us through a separate gate and into the baggage hall from where, we hoped, we would soon be going home.

How foolish were our thoughts!

Those of you who have also enjoyed coping with the frustrations of an airport's 'baggage handling problems' know what it's like when the carousels are not clearing.

We had to wait over an hour for our luggage to become available before we could each begin our journeys home.

By the way, my client's flight didn't stay routine either.

Initially, he had an uneventful flight and landed at a fog-free Jersey Airport. Additional passengers took their seats and the plane was being pushed back when, suddenly, it stopped and an announcement was made inviting passengers to evacuate the plane. Fortunately, not down the chutes but by steps that were quickly brought to two doorways where passengers safely disembarked – leaving their worldly possessions on the plane.

Apparently, an emergency dashboard light had illuminated and the captain had instantly aborted the flight. After engineers had made their inspection, and carried out tests, the bad news was that the plane was declared unfit to fly. However, the good news was that passengers were allowed back on board to collect their hand luggage and then wait for an alternative plane.

*Oh for the time when, like Captain Kirk in the Star Trek films and TV series, we will instantly teleport between locations. Each of our flight times was shorter than the delays in the airports!*

### Is that a BOGOF flight?

Having already been flying home for several hours, from Cape Town to London, we had had our meals and been put to bed – as they do on these overnight flights when the cabin crew want a quiet time – when we were awoken by the pilot announcing that he had to give us some bad news.

Whilst we had dozed, or slept, one of the engines had failed. As the plane probably did not have enough fuel to get all the way to Heathrow, and as there was nowhere that the engine could be repaired further on, he had decided to turn the plane around and so we would shortly be landing, at dawn, at Johannesburg, the nearest airport that could handle this type of emergency!

The landing on three engines was one of the smoothest my family and I had ever experienced, even though fire engines accompanied us down the runway. We disembarked and, as the repair was more complicated than expected, were taken to accommodation in hotels located at the airport. Apparently, only a certain type of engine would fit into our plane's structure.

Therefore, the maintenance crew had to wait for a plane with a compatible engine to arrive from New York and swop it for the faulty engine of our grounded plane. Eventually, very late that night, we took off again, and 11 hours later finally landed at Heathrow.

As we waited to be reunited with our luggage, we were confused to read, on the arrivals board, not only of the landing of our flight but also that of another plane from Cape Town – with the same flight number and touchdown time.

*As we made our way home, we wondered if it was from a parallel universe or if we had all travelled on the first of a pair of Buy-One-Get-One-Free flights.*

### THANK GOODNESS – ANOTHER EASY FLIGHT

I was booked on the last flight back to Heathrow, returning from a business meeting in Stuttgart, one January in the early 1980s. It was dark, very cold and snowing lightly. We boarded the plane, a Trident 3, and taxied out to the end of the runway. We sat there for a good ten minutes before the aircraft turned and taxied back to the terminal. The rear door opened and a couple of engineers entered and examined the inside of the rear engine compartment. They left the aircraft door open – it was freezing.

Eventually, the pilot informed us that the aircraft had not only the three standard engines of a Trident but that the Trident 3 also had a fourth booster engine at the rear. The fourth engine was fired like a rocket for a short period and was essential for take-off on short runways when carrying a full load.

Whilst on the runway, the pilot was only allowed to attempt to start the booster engine three times. If it did not start, after three attempts, the plane had to return to the terminal – Health & Safety regulations!

Yes, you've guessed it, Stuttgart had a short runway and we were carrying a full load.

The engineers could not find any fault with the booster engine, so the pilot informed us not to worry as he would jettison a couple of tons of freight from the hold and then we would be on our way.

An hour later, after the freight had been removed, the pilot informed us that, unfortunately, the weather conditions had changed and he had to lighten the plane load even more. As there was now no more freight to remove, he asked 12 passengers to volunteer to leave the aircraft for an 'all-expenses overnight stay in a Stuttgart Hotel'. I have to say it did not appeal to me, so, needless to say, I did not volunteer.

Now being 12 passengers lighter, the pilot then informed us that the weather conditions and wind direction had changed again but – not to worry – he was going to take off in the opposite direction.

We then proceeded to the other end of the runway, without the use of the booster engine, lighter by two tons of freight and the weight of 12 passengers.

We roared down the runway and rose swiftly into the sky. It seemed to me, as a seasoned traveller, that the booster engine had certainly lifted us off rather quickly. Moments later the pilot came on again and announced, 'That was an easy lift-off.'

**'Ummn,' I wondered. 'I don't think the passengers left behind would have agreed.'**

## NO! YOU CAN'T SHARE A SEAT! ...

### ... so someone has to be bribed!

It had been a frustrating week discussing with some 'Eurocrats' the intricacies of European radar systems. Consequently, I was extremely tired by the time I boarded the last flight back from the continent to the UK on this Friday evening.

Joining the queue of all male passengers up the steps and into the cabin, we all wondered what the delay was in people taking their seats. We then discovered that there were 31 passengers and it was only a 30-seat plane (and someone sitting on someone else's lap was not going to be allowed!)

The dispatch computer had issued one too many boarding passes. We knew that because everyone had to show them to the two cabin staff who were trying to resolve the problem of 'who sat where'.

As it was the last flight of the day back to London, and I'm sure all the travellers were as keen as the captain to return home, he decided to announce the following invitation to us all – in order to seek a passenger who would leave the plane and return on a Saturday morning flight.

He first offered free dinner and drinks – but no takers. He then added a free night at a local hotel to the dinner and drinks invitation – we all stood still or sat tight if we had a seat. The engines were running and I am sure we were all wondering what would happen next.

Then, up the landing steps and into the doorway came an airport 'Traffic Manager'. He repeated the pilot's offer, and then announced he would ensure that, this being Amsterdam – a companion from amongst the hotels' 'ladies of the night' would be available – if only someone would volunteer to leave the plane!

I've often wondered if the dark-suited businessman who immediately shouted out, 'I'll go' had to provide an explanation of the bribe he'd accepted to whomever was waiting for him that Friday night at Heathrow.

### Or, ultimately, sometime Saturday!

### ... the authorities won't allow this

Southend Airport on a weekday evening. I was on the last flight to Amsterdam in order to be in time for an early morning meeting the next day. The plane was full, nearly all the passengers being Dutch housewives who had had a good day shopping in this part of eastern England.

Two, who had obviously shared a couple of drinks (at least) before boarding, were somehow sitting on the same seat with only one boarding pass between them and neither would get off. They refused to obey the flight attendant, and then the instructions of the pilot. He, in turn, refused to take off until one of them left.

A local airport manager was called and he, too, was ignored. The women pretended not to understand and just sat there. Would they have to be removed forcibly I wondered? The problem was solved by the appearance of a Southend police sergeant. They took one look at him in his splendid uniform, complete with helmet and truncheon and both left the plane immediately.

*He hadn't needed to say a word, nor wave his truncheon!*

## TRAVELLERS – YOU HAVE BEEN WARNED!

The following tips have been kindly provided by someone who would know: A baggage handling manager for one of Britain's major airports. So take note of what follows. You have been warned!

### Advice to remember – or forget at your peril

Be careful to avoid packing anything in a soft bag or cardboard box. Such items may sometimes (surely will be) left out in the rain before loading. They then don't travel very well inside cargo containers.

If you happen to work for an airline, never, ever, tell your airport friends that you are flying from their airport. Your luggage will be found and 'nasty' things attached to its handles that will have to be explained on baggage collection, when all you really want to do is start your holiday!

Do not pack smelly food in your luggage. Whether the handlers enjoy its odour, or perhaps don't, it may sometimes be (probably will be) left in the hottest part of the airport before loading, so it will have gained an extra 'tang' at your arrival destination. That can help excite the new furry friends (sniffer dogs) that may be waiting to greet you.

For 'security reasons', bags that are making a buzzing sound will be opened, no matter what locks are on them. It is usually the case that an electric razor has switched itself on. However, any sex toys found will be prominently displayed in a clear plastic bag with your name on. Either this bag will end up going round on the luggage carousel at your destination, or will need to be asked for at the baggage desk. Either way, you may be too embarrassed to collect it.

'Heavy loads' will nearly always miss flights as 'Health & Safety' regulations require two people to load them and it is not always possible to find two people – in any loading area – available at the same time!

Don't expect initiative to be used when your luggage is handled. If your suitcase has tags from another flight left on it, your bag could (certainly would) return to that location, or anywhere else, instead of where you are now!

Last but not least:

**Luggage marked 'fragile' will NEVER be treated with the extra care this word requests.**

*Following on from those excitements, a seasoned traveller now recalls a variety of challenges he enjoyed whilst travelling for business. We learn why his blood pressure readings were never low whilst he was flying.*

## WHO SAID FLYING WASN'T EXCITING OR TIRING?

### Excitements whilst taking off

Three attempts to take off in a Trident at Heathrow before they decided to switch us to another aircraft. Two of them got us as far as the end of the runway awaiting clearance, on the third try the engines were at full power and the aircraft rolling, before the brakes were applied – very hard – and we taxied back, to change planes.

Two occasions when the pilot aborted take-off, braking to a stop within metres of the end of the runway, one of them the old Oslo Airport where the sea was waiting for us at the end of the runway – and looking very cold!

One 'brakes-full-on' due to a large bird flying into an engine of the BAE 146 just as we were about to lift off.

### In-Flight excitement

Three times struck by lightning whilst in the air climbing through cloud. Twice in Boeing 747s to Jakarta and Bangkok. Once in a Boeing 737 to Hamburg. (What is it with a Boeing?)

One person died in a seat across the aisle from me. A stewardess sat with the body for the remainder of the flight trying to remain nonchalant as I, and other nearby passengers, tried to avoid his fixed appearance.

One aborted landing resulting in us going round again into Munich.

This is an airport notorious for an approach close to the mountains, so, by the time we landed, all on board had really fast heartbeats!

(This traveller and the author both recall another approach route that helped keep your blood pressure up and, we imagine, that of the pilots. This was into Kai Tak*, the original airport at Hong Kong that closed in 1998. On occasions, you definitely went near, as well as over, residents' clothes hanging on washing lines on the balconies of the blocks of flats nearby the airport. So close, in fact, it seemed like you could read the labels in their shirts and blouses. It was also exciting when it was the Monsoon season as the rain made the tarmac very slippery. You just hoped the plane you were on would stop before it skidded off the end of the runway – and nose-dived into the harbour!)

*Search the internet for You Tube films of landings at Kai Tak.

### A more serious excitement

One MAYDAY incident as a passenger in a twin-engine Cessna halfway across the channel from France. One engine began losing fuel causing a loss of power from the second engine. Insufficient fuel remained to make it to the UK on the good engine, but just enough – thankfully – to allow us to turn around and divert back to Cherbourg.

### And some excitements I have luckily missed

No nights spent sleeping at an airport due to missing a flight, not being able to get on a flight or having a flight cancelled at the last minute.*

*The author of this book has not been so lucky having, on two occasions, been abandoned at an airport when they were shutting down due to severe weather and snowstorms. He can particularly confirm that the floor inside the bar of the Sheraton Hotel at Terminal Two of Charles de Gaulle Airport is especially uncomfortable and very tiring to try to get to sleep on.

Gaining a corner spot amongst the hundred or so 'campers' awaiting rescheduled flights to various locations, he was also disappointed to learn that the kitchen had run out of food, such had been the demand by passengers similarly abandoned!

**However, conversation and a 'United Nations' camaraderie was certainly helped by the draught beer remaining 'on tap'.**

## WILL WE GO ALL THE WAY?

I was visiting the southern Appalachians and, as the Cherohala Skyway Highway was not far off route to the airport home, Charlotte in North Carolina, I thought that would be an interesting diversion. Besides being very twisty, the road rose to 5,000 feet above sea level and involved driving through cloud and across occasional patches of snow.

Despite my valiant (and high speed) effort on the interstates, I still missed my departure check-in by 20 minutes. Nevertheless, the desk staff were great, checking out various routes to get me back to the UK, but their efforts were hampered by the fact that the best choice, Newark International Airport, was about to close due to an anticipated heavy snowstorm.

However, they got me on an internal hopper flight to Newark, and next evening I managed to board the 'red-eye' plane to London but we had to wait 25 minutes whilst the ground staff de-iced the plane before it started taxiing. I became apprehensive when the pilot, who could have chosen better words, announced,

**'That should be enough de-icing to get us to the end of the runway.'
I had ambitions to go further!**

## 6)   TRAVEL – IT REALLY DOES BROADEN THE MIND

The title of this chapter highlights one of the benefits of travel. As the author T S Eliot said, 'It's the journey not the arrival that matters.' Those of us who have coped with cancelled or missed flights might think otherwise.

Similarly, those who have enjoyed some interesting taxi journeys (whether at home or abroad) might feel a tinge of nostalgia when they look back. But I don't think a fast pulse rate, gained from experiencing the driver's swift and skilful (?) driving, are what we really want when we go to a new country or location, whether on business or for a holiday.

As you will already have read in an earlier chapter, you may be challenged to confirm where you are from. Discussing this location and the performance of any Premier League football club the taxi driver may support will certainly break the ice and help smooth your journey.

Unfortunately, in my experience, you will rarely agree on which team, or footballer, is the best.

*Newspaper headings and notices to get you thinking …*

ATHLETE'S FOOT STORE OPENS IN SHOPPING MALL IN LISBON, PORTUGAL
*Will customers really want to go and buy that fungus?*

MINERS REFUSE TO WORK AFTER DEATH
*Good-for-nothing, lazy so-and-sos!*

In a laundry in Rome
LADIES, LEAVE YOUR CLOTHES HERE AND SPEND THE AFTERNOON HAVING A GOOD TIME
*La Dolce Vita?*

Sign on the scaffolding around the site of a new hotel in Shandong, China
A NEW SWIMMING POOL IS RAPIDLY TAKING SHAPE AS BEHIND THIS SCREEN WE HAVE THROWN IN THE BULK OF OUR WORKERS

NINJA TURTLE? NO, A CHINESE SMUGGLER'S SANDWICH!
Airport security guards in South East China have caught a man attempting to smuggle his pet turtle onto an aeroplane inside a KFC hamburger. He was stopped at the x-ray machines in Guangzhou Airport when unusual 'protrusions' were seen poking out of a sandwich inside his bag.
Forced to hand over his 'lunch' he continued the journey without his friend / meal.

## AN ENGLISHMAN ABROAD

Have you ever been, like me, the 'piggy-in-the-middle' between French and German businessmen arguing over who knows best? If so, you too may have found Germans to be rather tense and the French very resistant to change. This has often led to entrenched positions during negotiations or, in my case, resistance to the process I was inviting both nationalities to adopt, one where the feedback of the end-users (of the services they had provided to them) was to be considered sacrosanct. Not so, according to the German and French aerospace engineers. They knew best – the customers were wrong!

Enter an Englishman, believing four principles:

1) Don't take yourself too seriously.

2) Don't take anything too seriously.

3) Try and avoid confrontation.

4) A difficult situation needs diffusing with some humour.

However, I always found the last principle the hardest to apply as everyone concerned views humour in a different way. So, a fifth principle was often implemented. Take a break and drink the beverage that Englishmen knew would most refresh; a nice cup of tea!

There was another reason why this approach could have been personally successful. At the time of this particular process challenge, I had thought of setting this group of difficult international staff the team-building task of redesigning the teapot I had at home. Regardless of who used it, my wife and I found it always poured most of the contents onto the tray and just a little into our teacups.

There I was with a group of engineers who had designed the world's largest passenger plane (the A380). Solving my problem would surely have been possible by such experts. Then I realised, of course, that they were all coffee drinkers, so would never have enjoyed the problem anyway, and might have started arguing even more.

## ARE WE THERE YET?

The annual holiday for the family had generally been in England and, although limited by the weather, had been largely successful over the years. However, my wife and I now felt that, as the children were older, it would be good to travel further and perhaps take advantage of the sunnier possibilities of continental Europe.

Preparations for the annual event were always tedious and the car was frequently loaded and unloaded several times before the maximum amount of items were compressed into the minimum amount of space. This particular year's packing was even more memorable as I had paid special attention to cleaning and polishing my newly purchased Vauxhall Cavalier Mark 1 in preparation for an early start the next day.

The car shone and sparkled in the bright sunshine of the summer's day and, to enjoy the full effect of the car's elegant lines, I slammed shut the boot and stood back to admire my handiwork.

Disaster! The locked boot now contained the only set of car keys. I phoned the local dealership but they seemed particularly unhelpful about replacement keys. It was several hours later, and after much conversation with my family, that I was ready to pack the car again having drilled through the lock, removed the cases, cleaned-up the pieces of broken lock from the boot, driven ten miles to and from the dealer, purchased a replacement lock and keys, returned home and fitted the new lock.

The only good thing about this exciting experience was that the ferry crossing was not until the next morning from the port of Dover …

***… so I had the chance to admire my handiwork and initiative, and take the praise (?) of my family!***

## AT LEAST ONE DELEGATE SMILED AT ME

I had been invited to lecture during a week's MBA programme in Nicosia, Cyprus, for the Cypriot Institute of Management. My session was on Wednesday morning, by when the 50 or so delegates had melded into a group and I was certainly an outsider. However, I did know the course leader very well and, after introducing me at 9.00 am, he returned to sit at the back of the large conference room to welcome any latecomers (which was to be expected) and to observe how the group responded to my concepts and questions.

The conference room was laid out in the traditional U-shape with several rows and a central aisle that led from the entrance door to the centre of the stage. The desk where my notes and I were positioned was to one side, so that I could look at both the slides on the screen, which was on the stage, and the audience sitting in front of me.

At about 10.00 am, the doors opened and an attractive young lady, very smartly dressed in a suede business suit, opened the door. She was greeted by my friend and invited to sit at the back of the hall, but in a row just in front of him.

I did not refer to her arrival, carrying on with my sequence of slides, focusing on the whole group and keeping a watchful eye on the clock at the back of the room, as we usually stopped at 10.45 am for a coffee break.

However, as that time approached, my friend handed the young lady a note and then came to the front of the room carrying a similar piece of folded notepaper that he handed to me. He returned promptly to the back in order to watch my reaction. I assumed I would read that the coffee was not ready and I should continue past 11.00 am. Instead, I was extremely shocked to read the following message: 'Your zip is undone and we can see your panties and everything!'

Imagine my consternation at the thought that I'd been lecturing for over an hour in such a state of undress, especially as I had not been static by the desk but rather, paced across the room and passed close to the delegates in the first row.

At the same time as trying to continue my slideshow, I thought for a moment: 'Hold on, panties, I'm not wearing those' and I actually, and surreptitiously, felt that my trouser fly zip was completely fastened, so what on earth was the note about?

Rather than continue teaching, I announced, 'We'll be taking an early coffee break, as it seems it's already arrived.' (Luckily, I had seen movement outside the door.)

Walking briskly to the back of the room I showed my friend his note and asked, 'What on earth were you doing?' He seemed very perplexed and looking at the young lady in front of him, who was equally puzzled, asked her for her note. She had the one that said the coffee had arrived early!

We both confirmed, by looking at the back of the young lady's suit, the condition she was in. Luckily, he was able to whisper to her in Cypriot what was wrong and, without a moment's hesitation, she rushed from our gaze!

After an extended coffee break, the session was reconvened and the young lady sat back down (I assumed with her zip fastened) and gave me a smile that I can only describe as saying:

**'I now know what you know, and it can be a secret between us!'**

## BLAST, I'VE SEEN THIS FILM BEFORE

Our company was a major account for the local high street travel agency, with most arrangements being made by our secretaries. However, on one occasion, I had reason to telephone their offices and was told, after initial pleasantries, how nice it was to be talking directly to one of the company's senior travellers, and that we were one of the best companies in the town to deal with.

When I enquired what she meant, she explained that all the other companies had their staff telephone one or two days before the booked flight, demanding to know what film was going to be shown on the aircraft their executive would be flying on. If he had seen the film already, an alternative flight would be requested. This was in the 1980s when in-flight entertainment on flights to the US consisted of trying to watch a few overhead TV screens. These were hung down the central aisle, with the same film being shown throughout the plane, and you listened through small headphones that plugged into a socket at your seat.

**On several occasions after this conversation, I found myself having to travel at short notice and wishing I, too, had thought of asking about the film, instead of doing immediately as my boss wanted, with the result that I watched the same film more than once!**

## DON'T THEY NEED ALL THE PARTS OF THE ENGINE TO MAKE OUR PLANE FLY?

In the mid-1990s, I was to take an internal flight on an Air China plane to Shandong province with a colleague, who had, I was soon to learn, a weak heart. Arriving at the local and very small airport to board the plane, we found we had some time to wait, as there was a delay 'due to an engine problem with our plane'.

(We only learned that by chance as the one other European in the departure lounge spoke good Mandarin and caught the Tannoy announcement that we were in for a wait of several hours. We needn't have worried as we were soon to learn of it for ourselves in a rather, certainly to my colleague, stressful way.)

No sooner were we sitting down, expecting hours of boredom, than a team of ground crew/engineers in clean and bright blue overalls proceeded to pull an open hand cart – which we could see had nothing in it other than boxes of tools – through our lounge and out of the double doors, adjacent to where this plane was parked on the runway. I told you it was a very small airport.

Intrigued, the three of us got up and watched as they proceeded to climb onto the wings and dismantle the cowling of, presumably, the faulty engine. After a while, our interest died down, and we returned to our seats to discuss how we were going to cope with missed connections later in the trip.

Picture our anxiety, and certainly that of my colleague, when from our fellow traveller, listening to another announcement, we learnt that the plane was ready to fly – much earlier than we were expecting.

This consternation was triggered by the fact that, as soon as the announcement had finished, the outer doors opened and the engineers and their cart returned, retracing their route past our seats.

All three of us could not help but notice that they had made no effort to cover up the various parts of the engine that the cart now contained. We certainly agreed that those bits weren't there when they went out to the plane, so they must have come from the engine they intended to use to take off with!

At this point, my colleague had a turn for the worse and, with the help of the other traveller, I was able to calm him down, ensure he took his Angina medication (which I didn't know he carried everywhere) and generally consider our situation.

Such was his keenness to get back to 'civilisation' that he said we must get on the plane 'whatever the consequences'. Personally, I didn't think they were worth thinking about!

As we boarded, even I wondered if I should ask for one of his tablets when, as a gesture of apology, the single cabin crew member presented each of us with two Air China silk ties and a ball point pen as gifts to apologise for the delay.

Luckily – otherwise I wouldn't be writing this – the plane flew us to our destination. I often used the pen and wore one of the ties on future trips, and, every time I flew with Air China …

**… *I hoped the same team had not serviced the plane I was on and that its engines contained all the components they required.***

## DON'T WORRY, WE WON'T SHOOT YOU

If you travel to Schiphol Airport in Amsterdam and, upon arrival, need a taxi, you have to go outside and join the queue at the very efficiently organised taxi rank. I was well used to this method and moved slowly forward, amongst other businessmen, pushing my suitcase in front of me and awaiting my pickup at the official point.

One of the constant streams of smart Mercedes cars pulled alongside me and the driver flipped the boot lid up. I placed my case in it and then immediately sat on the back seat, about to tell him the location of my hotel.

Imagine my shock, and his, as four armed, plainclothes policemen, showing their handguns and warrant cards, surrounded the car shouting in Dutch and English that the driver was to get out and I was to stay put!

This was not long after the tragic events of the London Bombings of 7 July 2005, so I hope you can imagine how fast my pulse was racing. I thought I looked innocent and business-like – but who knows?

Once the driver was standing on the pavement and being handcuffed, the policeman next to my door opened it politely, and asked me to step out. He then explained that I had unwittingly sat in an unmarked and unlicensed car, supposedly offering itself as an official taxi.

Apparently, this was a large, organised scam at the airport and the authorities had decided to put an end to it. Unfortunately, various criminal gangs from Eastern Europe were masterminding it and there had been previous dangerous instances. He told me they had, therefore, decided to take no risks in future so, as a policy, always showed their weapons.

While I was still calming down, one of his colleagues, also politely, had hailed an official taxi and made it quite clear that I was not to be charged a fare. The driver had already been given an official ticket to cover my costs and never told me whether he was part of the police operation or not.

*I didn't mind. I used the taxi fare I hadn't spent on buying myself a large brandy, once I had checked into my hotel – to calm my still shaking nerves.*

## FEARFUL IN-FLIGHT ENTERTAINMENT

As you will have read in the earlier story, 'Blast, I've seen this film before' flying long haul in the 'good old days' meant that the most passengers got to watch was a movie, projected from a video machine, onto a screen at the front of each section of cabin. Whilst the following anecdote comes from a different contributor, and relates to flying in the 1990s, in-flight projection technology was still pretty basic. Video player machines were temperamental enough in our homes, let alone when they were being flown at 30,000 feet.

On this particular flight, I actually had a seat that allowed me to watch easily whatever films were showing, as it was at the front of the economy seats, adjacent to the galley service area.

I watched with bemusement, or was it mild apprehension, as the time for the first screening arrived and several of the cabin staff, then the second flying officer, tried to get the video player, located in the wall of the service area, switched on.

After much button pushing, the officer removed the whole door panel to the cabinet that housed the projection equipment and started banging on the video machine inside.

I never knew whether it was the force of his attack, or just an untimely coincidence but, at that moment, all the lights in the cabin went out!

I turned and remarked to a fellow passenger, 'Let's hope this video technician hasn't turned off all the flying controls as well.'

**The look on his face suggested he thought I might be telling the truth!**

Postscript: I'm pleased to say that, after five minutes, the lights came back on and the film began. Otherwise, I might not be here telling you about the event.

## FRENCH DRIVING IS GOOD FOR RAISING YOUR BLOOD PRESSURE

It was evening and the new and enthusiastic French sales representative for our company, François, who was now driving us across Paris, had picked the three of us up from our hotel.

He was keen to update us with all his recent business opportunities and so kept up an almost constant explanation, during which he felt compelled to keep turning round to the two of us in the rear of the car, gesticulating at the same time – as many Frenchmen like to do.

Travelling down the Rue de Rivoli past the Louvre, we drove through one set of traffic lights at red, then another and were showing no signs of stopping at the third set that was looming up. François, in the meantime, was becoming more and more animated.

At this point, my colleague in the front passenger seat of the car, who up until this time had not been speaking much, asked in a superb English accent and with no trace of apprehension, 'What particular shade of red are you looking for François?'

*This did the trick in a diplomatic way and we all relaxed, François slowed down and we survived the rest of the journey without incident.*

## FRESH MEAT FOR BREAKFAST?

An early morning jogger was apprehended and brought back to the safety of the Keekorok Lodge, a protected and usually peaceful compound in the middle of the Masai Mara National Reserve, where my wife and I were staying. During an argument in the reception, which our tour party watched, he protested that he was a fit young male with years of running experience, braving the South Side of Chicago.

He also explained that he had taken the extraordinary precaution of arming himself with a handy and versatile Swiss Army knife. This, he assured the security staff, would have dealt swiftly with any of the fierce creatures that had set up shop around the compound, eagerly anticipating the sight of a 'Muzungu' (the southern, central and eastern African term for a 'person of European descent').

His bravado faded when he was told that, only a month earlier, a similarly hapless jogger had been less fortunate.

*He was not only seen, he had become breakfast for a pride of lions.*

## I COULDN'T BE CHOOSY ABOUT WHERE MY HAIR WAS CUT, OR ITS STYLE

Having your hair cut in both the cities and rural areas of China was always an exciting event to those with any sensitivity about where it was going to happen and who might be watching. Often, the barber was occupying nothing more than an area of the pavement, perhaps surrounded on three sides by some sort of sheeting, put there only to stop the cut hair blowing about in the wind. Invariably, the chosen location was at the side of a major crossroads, so everyone could see the barber (?) was available for business.

The sophistication of the 'salon' experience consisted of sitting on the equivalent of a cheap dining room chair and watching the residents go by on their bicycles, in buses or taxis. Of course, whilst they watched the traffic lights, they also studied how you, as a Westerner, were reacting to such a public event.

These haircuts were never the occasion to display any annoyance towards those stares, to choose anything sophisticated in terms of a style (the traditional very short back and sides seemed to be de rigueur), or to refuse to take part in the general discussion that inevitably occurred with both the people passing by, and those standing waiting for their own haircuts.

*As these conversations were always in Mandarin, I was never sure if they were talking at me – or more likely – about me!*

## I'LL GIVE YOUR JACKET A CERTIFICATE – NOT YOU!

One of my responsibilities, whilst working on the World Bank project in Tianjin, was to present a series of workshops describing western management techniques.

Each of these had to be held between the hours of 9.00 am and 5.00 pm exactly, as well as very carefully structured to suit the importance of the delegates, usually the most senior executives of each factory in a particular industry. Of course, they were also to be presented in Mandarin, using my interpreter, and supported by both handouts of the slides and a certificate of attendance.

The World Bank, which was funding this activity, also required a register, listing the names and job titles of those present, so as to validate both the certificate and certain stage payments in the project timetable.

These events always occurred in the boardrooms of the factories, so that the executives could visit their offices during the slightly extended lunch hour.

This particular meeting opened with the usual pleasantries and business card exchange activity (an essential courtesy when meeting for the first time), and I began to explain the topics to be covered that day.

Sitting at the front of the group, on the right-hand side, nearest to the room's main door, I noticed, out of the corner of my eye, that the delegate there was already removing his jacket and slipping it over the back of his chair. Then he removed his glasses, carefully positioning them, his delegate pack and a fountain pen in the centre of the blotter laid in front of him.

No sooner had he finished this elaborate ritual than the door opened and a Chinese lady, presumably his secretary, crept, without looking at me, into the room and whispered something to this executive.

He promptly got up, also not looking at me, turned smartly round and went out of the room, taking her with him, but leaving behind his jacket on the back of his chair, and glasses, pack and pen on the blotter.

Mentally, I assumed he would be returning in a short while, so continued my presentation rather than stop and wait for him.

It was just as well I carried on as he did not return during the morning's break for refreshments, nor for the lunch laid out on a long table at the back of the room, nor during the afternoon break.

In fact, I saw no more of him until ten minutes before 5.00 pm. Then, the door opened and he walked smartly in and resumed his seat.

It was at this time that I was closing the workshop and beginning to invite each delegate to the front to receive their attendance certificate. Each one of these was a carefully named document, which I had had to sign during the afternoon's break.

I had begun with the person sitting on the left-hand side of the boardroom table and worked my way around the group until the delegate, who had been absent for the entire meeting, was the last one left.

He rose, slipped his jacket on, picked up his pen, pack and glasses expecting me to call him forward, but I didn't, instead I spoke to my interpreter and asked him to explain, quietly in Mandarin, that I would see this gentleman after everyone had left. Immediately, I could sense there was tension in the air, especially when my nervous interpreter pleaded with me to make the presentation as I was inviting the executive to lose face.

I refused, brought the meeting to an end and invited all those who had a certificate to leave the room.

I then explained to this very annoyed delegate that I was not prepared to issue a certificate to someone who had not been present during the day, only leaving his jacket on the back of his chair to give the impression he was there - which he said he had been – and I said he was definitely not!

I knew I was creating a diplomatic incident so made a point of immediately telephoning our local project office to explain what had happened.

It was just as well I did for, next morning, I was summoned to the Regional World Bank office, on the other side of the city, and asked to explain why I had insulted a senior manager of the plant.

Fortunately, the office director accepted my explanation, so much so that I later learnt the manager had been demoted, as it was felt he had not only insulted me but also the whole concept of the development programme.

This was reinforced, when I held subsequent workshops at this plant, by the refusal of any of his ex-colleagues to sit in that same chair, or remove their jackets, or leave the room during the time I was talking.

**It was as if they were sensing that his spirit, if not his person, was definitely still in the room.**

## INTO THE LION'S DEN – A NOVICE BITES INTO THE BIG APPLE

When I first started as a global business warrior, it began with trips to headquarters in New York. The first ever trip was in the company of my boss of the time, somebody who had travelled the world for a good number of years. As a result, I trundled behind him in awe of his stories about The Big Apple.

My problems started on my second trip that took me there on my own. Arriving at JFK Airport, late on a Sunday evening, I struggled through the notorious US immigration to be faced with a huge queue for a yellow cab into Manhattan.

A guy appeared, walking up and down the queue, offering a cab into Manhattan. This seemed a way to jump the queue and, as time was tight before my meeting, was just what I needed, so off I went with him. Walking to his car, he showed me a printed price list of all the hotels and a set price.

Arriving at the car, the first warning bell rang – no yellow cab, just a private car. OK, I thought, obviously a guy moonlighting. Still, what did I care as long as he was charging me the standard fare? So off we went and duly arrived at the right hotel in Manhattan. All sorted, I paid my $90 and checked in for a good night's sleep!

The next day I arrived at the office, duly refreshed, and commenced a full day of meetings. During lunch, a local colleague (another Brit working for our US firm) told the story of his 80 year old mother who had recently visited his family in NY, arriving on her own.

He had warned her that the yellow cabs were heavily regulated and there was a fixed fare into Manhattan, at about $30! The driver had tried to charge her $60 but she had raised hell with him for trying to swindle an old lady and a tourist to boot! I kept my mouth shut, realising my $90 'bargain' was far from being so … whoops!

Back home it's now time to submit my travel expenses. Do I swallow the cost or claim? Honesty being the best policy, I submitted the claim with a narrative explaining what had happened. The partner in charge roared with laughter at the obvious embarrassment I was experiencing, but thankfully, he signed it off.

*This was accompanied by the statement that it had happened to everyone, but only once, for the company would not reimburse us for our innocence another time.*

## SUICIDE AND FLOWER POWER, AN INTERESTING COMBINATION

It was some 20 years ago, during one of my trips with my company's Egyptian agent, when I felt I was in the company of someone wishing to commit suicide. He drove his Mercedes at its maximum speed through the downtown area of Cairo, violating systematically all traffic rules as if these were not designed for him.

At my question, whether he was afraid of being stopped and given a heavy speeding fine, the answer was clear. This situation could not be a problem as he had arranged that, once a year, the police would combine all the fines, invite him to a police station and then amicably negotiate an amount to settle the outstanding sums. He considered this a very rewarding arrangement since the time saved during the year enabled him to earn a multiple of whatever sum of money was agreed.

After a near miss at a traffic light, where he could not avoid stopping, a young boy of about seven years old approached him with some flowers in his hand, with the clear intention of selling them to my agent. Winding down his car's front off-side window and having some discussion in Arabic, the agent laughed, paid the youngster some money for the flowers and handed them to me. I asked him what he was smiling about.

He explained that the flowers I was holding first grew in the spring, when they had a great fragrance. They flowered again in late summer, which is the time I'm remembering, but without any scent.

However, the bunch he had just purchased certainly did. We both could smell it.

Apparently, the youngster had a canister of cheap perfume that he sprayed over the flowers – just before selling them. My agent said that this type of commercial enterprise deserved a good reward, and a tip. I suggested this was not the sort of practice we should consider applying to the sale of our products.

**_He looked crestfallen, for he had obviously thought of doing just that!_**

## WOULD SIR LIKE A ROOM SERVICE EXTRA?

Many years ago, when I was working for the major commercial insurance division of an international Risk Management brokers, we were appointed to manage the Clarks Shoes account. At this time, they had about 25 factories spread around the West Country of England and their head office, main plant and the original factory were in Street in Somerset

I was sent to visit all of the factories, together with a Fire Surveyor, to gather information about the business and to assess their insurance risks. We were to start at Street and booked ourselves into the hotel there that was opposite the company's headquarters. Clarks owned this accommodation and it turned out that it was 'dry' and so did not serve any alcohol! There were no public houses in the town either, and as Clarks owned just about everything – the houses, the electricity supply, the milkman, shops and so on – there was little chance of finding any liquor anywhere.

(Josiah Clark, the founder of the company, was a Quaker and a friend of other notable Quakers of the time such as John Cadbury, of chocolate fame and Robert Barclay, founder of Barclays Bank. Whilst Josiah was a philanthropic employer, he was also a strict teetotaller.)

Anyway, we stayed at the hotel, which was an old-fashioned, smallish place, and on the first morning at 7.00 am, I was brought a tray of tea in bed. The very comely young maid, who set it down, knowingly looked at me and then said in her broad Somerset accent 'Sir, if you would like, that tea could cost you £10!'

I was nonplussed but in the best traditions of (say?) newspaper reporters, I declined her kind offer. I drank the tea, bathed, dressed, and went down to breakfast. However, my young colleague arrived much later, smiling broadly, and only had time for a slice of toast!

**_I was sure I knew why he was late and he knew I knew why, but we did not share our thoughts!_**

## YOU LIKE A MESSAGE OR A MASSAGE?

I had been making business trips to an electronics company in Guangdong (formerly Canton), a coastal province of southeast China that borders Hong Kong and Macau, for several years. Its capital, Guangzhou, sits within its industrial Pearl River Delta region. This sprawling port city is home to the octagonal Sun Yat-sen Memorial Hall, commemorating the founder of modern China. As such, the city has many different and varied hotels that cater for both Chinese visitors and international tourists wanting to visit the port or the commemorative exhibition in the hall.

After a hard day negotiating a contract, the various dishes of the celebratory dinner, and the associated mixtures of Chinese wine and beer, I was glad to get to bed, and immediately fell asleep.

Roused somewhat crossly by the telephone on the dressing table of my bedroom continually ringing, I answered it and listened to the night porter, on the front desk, telling me there was a message for me.

When he explained it needed to be brought to my room, I agreed and waited sleepily for the doorbell to ring. It did and no sooner had I opened the door than a young Chinese lady pushed past me beginning to take off her clothes and saying she'd come to give me the massage!

You will have to believe me when I say I pushed her brusquely out of the room, slammed the door and then rang reception, and 'gave them a piece of my mind'.

When checking out in the morning, I discovered that this was a standard trick by the night staff to earn a little money on the side …

*… and it was my fault that I had muddled up two similar sounding words!*

## 7)   *LIFE IS STRANGER THAN FICTION*

We've been a little economical with the truth in using this heading. Mark Twain actually said 'Truth is stranger than fiction, but it is because Fiction is obliged to stick to possibilities; Truth isn't.' We hope you'll bear that thought in mind as you enjoy the examples that follow. We couldn't really invent the actual situations being described in this chapter; they are all true.

Perhaps we've all assumed, when arriving somewhere supposedly posh, that all the requisite toiletries and accommodation arrangements will be in place. Unfortunately, this was not the case in the story 'Bring your own towel and soap next time!' This example shows it's not much fun when your expectations are unfulfilled. Perhaps you, too, have enjoyed a similar disappointment.

Postscript: Readers wanting more examples of life being stranger than anything that can be imagined should seek out copies of the book, 'Ripley's Believe it or not', Ripley Publishing Ltd.

*Newspaper headings and notices that amaze or perplex …*

PANDA MATING FAILS; VETERINARIAN TAKES OVER
*What a hero! Will he also eat bamboo shoots?*

A question that might challenge some who saw it on a poster in 'downtown' Johannesburg:
ARE YOU AN ADULT THAT CANNOT READ? IF SO WE CAN HELP

On the wall of a Californian restaurant:
CUSTOMERS WHO FIND OUR WAITRESSES RUDE OUGHT TO MEET THE MANAGER

Hotel room card, Istanbul:
BECAUSE OF THE IMPROPRIETY OF ENTERTAINING GUESTS OF THE OPPOSITE SEX IN THE BEDROOM, IT IS SUGGESTED THAT THE LOBBY BE USED FOR THIS PURPOSE

A special service offered in a hotel in Poland:
THE FLATTENING OF YOUR UNDERWEAR WITH PLEASURE IS THE JOB OF THE CHAMBERMAID

SOMETHING WENT WRONG IN JET CRASH, EXPERT SAYS
*Really? That's what usually happens.*

HAVE YOU EVER SEEN TABLE MAGIC?
This is where professional magicians circulate amongst the tables at a dinner in order to entertain and amaze guests, and camouflage the time it's taking to serve the meals. If so, have you wondered how they can produce £20 notes, or even higher value ones, from under your napkin or bread plate - whilst wearing dinner jackets and dress shirts with the sleeves cut off at the elbows, and with their hands (supposedly) empty - when there's, seemingly, nowhere to hide the money?

I saw this at a city dinner and did just wonder if, during the daytime, the magicians might be working for the Bank of England and, whilst there, creating – as if from thin air – new money for the government policy known as Quantitative Easing, an unconventional form of Central Bank monetary policy much loved by politicians.

## ALL THAT GLITTERS ISN'T GOLD

At one stage of my life, I had to investigate insurance claims and decide whether the claimants should receive settlement money for the loss of, or damage to, their property. This would often involve having one-to-one sessions with the claimants, who came from all over the world to present their cases.

A particular individual from one of the Arab states was claiming for the loss of around £2,500 and, luckily for him, I was able to pay his claim on the same day. He was extremely grateful. A few days later, he returned to my office to reward me personally for my time and courtesy. I had to explain I could not accept any personal gifts. However, he was most insistent and told me in his country it would be an insult to refuse. He then brought out a folder from his briefcase, which contained a variety of gold coins of different sizes all in individual plastic wallets, and asked me to pick out any two.

I have to admit I chose two of the largest ones, but again refused to accept them. At that he said, 'I will leave them on your desk and you can do what you like with them.' He then left. I looked at these two crown-sized gold coins for a while, contemplating what I would do with them. Eventually, I greedily picked them up to feel their weight, only to find they were as light as feathers, something similar to old-fashioned Italian coins with little metal content, and covered with cheap gold-type paint.

**Was his claim genuine? I still don't know, but those 'gold coins' were definitely fake and I was gullible to accept his kindness.**

## ARE THOSE GUYS VIPs OR SPECIAL AGENTS?

Having finished a business trip in the USA, in the early 1980s, a colleague and I were dropped off at JFK Airport, New York for the flight back to the UK. We had around five hours before departure. As my colleague had never seen Manhattan before, we were, luckily, able to check in our bags early and catch a city bus for a quick glimpse of the 'Big Apple'.

We believed the trip would be easy and the service reliable, but a deluge suddenly descended from the skies and, within a very short time, the traffic ground to a halt. The rain then continued unabated.

After about an hour of little progress, we began thinking that we would need to catch the return bus as soon as we reached our destination, Times Square. After another hour, it was clear that we were not even going to reach Manhattan with enough time left to return to the airport.

By now, the bus was somewhere in the badlands of New York, moving just a few yards at a time, so we decided that the only way to get back to the airport in time was by the New York City metro train, but where was an underground station?

We got off the vehicle, having been assured by the driver that a station was 'over there somewhere' and, as we walked towards it, we sought help from the occasional passer-by.

Eventually, we located the station, which had the appearance of having sustained a strike by a missile, and waited on the platform, during which time there were up to a dozen rats at any one instant foraging among the tracks, oblivious of the crowd just above them.

The metro delivered us, somewhat anxiously, to JFK about five minutes before the scheduled take-off time. We had been hoping that the bad weather would have delayed the flight. However, it was not the weather but we ourselves who were threatening to cause a delay.

From the British Airways desk we were swiftly escorted – as if we were VIPs – through unknown areas of the airport terminal, bypassing security and normal passport control and ushered onto the aircraft and into our seats to the curious stares of the already seated, and intrigued, passengers.

We felt sure they were asking themselves, 'Are these guys just late or, instead, are they something special?' Perhaps then wondering if it was the completion of an undercover special agent assignment, which we had timed to perfection, in order to allow our escape at the last possible moment. Whichever, we never let on to those around us.

Mentioning this incident to our New York Office colleagues a day or two later, we were assured that in the area where we boarded the metro, we were indeed lucky to have emerged unscathed.

*Apparently, that special mission fantasy was not too far wrong.*

## BRING YOUR OWN TOWEL AND SOAP NEXT TIME!

A management consultant colleague sent me, late at night, to the officers' mess of a Royal Air Force station at Locking, a small town just outside Weston-super-Mare in Somerset. It was home to the RAF's No 1 Radio School, where we were to make a presentation next morning to the commanding officer and his senior team.

After a stressful day in our office getting ready for this important meeting, I was unprepared for what I subsequently experienced. Entering quite a Spartan bedroom, I found that not only did the curtains not reach the bottom of the windows, they didn't even close, no towel or soap was provided and the bed blankets looked particularly itchy.

Not having been a member of her Majesty's Armed Forces, instead being used to soft three or four star hotel living, it was all a bit of a shock. This was compounded by my hunger and thirst, having worked through my lunch hour and having got straight in the car to travel some hours down a major motorway to the defence site. Then, on entering the officers' mess, being told I was an unaccompanied civilian without an officer present 'to sign me in', so I could not purchase food or alcohol at the bar, did not put me in the best of moods.

Returning to my 'quarters' I decided I'd have a shower in the hope that this would help me to relax and I'd have a good night's sleep. I thought these items being available in the shower block would remedy the absence of any soap and toiletries in my bedroom.

Unfortunately, this was not the case and I certainly wasn't brave enough to ask the person – with the very shapely, non-hairy, female looking legs, that I could see below the plastic curtain of one of the two cubicles – if she had any.

Being an honourable gentleman (believe me, if you will), I immediately vacated the area and returned to my bedroom in order to telephone my colleague and ask what the (expletive deleted) was I supposed to do?

Fortunately, he lived about an hour away and, although I didn't know it until the morning when I read a note pushed onto my room's entrance mat, he had driven to the base, hung wash items on the outside handle of my bedroom door, and then returned to his home.

When Vic retired he wanted
to have his home nearer the
coast. This was easy after
he aquired a light house.

Propertunity,
Sold

After my morning shower, this time with no one else around, I at last felt fresh and bright to face the challenge of the forthcoming meeting. However, I was not quite there yet. On entering the very large dining room attached to the officers' mess, I collected a thoughtfully provided newspaper lying on a table by the door and then chose a corner seat – to be out of the way of the various personnel arriving, like me, for their breakfast.

Enjoying a Full English and a leisurely read, my attention was broken by a commotion at the door. A tall, distinguished Army officer, wearing a peaked cap, was berating the waiter, demanding to know why I was sitting in his chair and reading his paper!

After the previous night's excitements, I thought I would just keep my head down and play dumb. Luckily, that worked and then, in the nick of time, my colleague arrived and, after my brief explanation of what was now happening, quickly escorted me away from my breakfast and the very unhappy Brigadier.

Luckily for us, this officer was not in the meeting we subsequently had, nor did the commanding officer, who chaired it, have a report about my misbehaviour either at breakfast or in the shower block the night before. This was surprising as, due to my frustration and tiredness, my friend told me I had entered the female shower block!

The meeting actually went extremely well, we were invited back many times to the base, I always remembered to take a towel, a bar of soap and newspaper and to get permission to visit the officers' mess on my own.

Postscript: Before our second visit, my colleague carefully informed me that an officer wearing his cap at breakfast was a traditional Army signal, to all around him, that he was not to be disturbed.

**The one whose seat I sat in, and newspaper I borrowed, was certainly interrupted that morning!**

## DON'T SET FIRE TO THE RESTAURANT, WE HAVEN'T EATEN YET

I was enjoying a quiet pint of beer and a read of my newspaper whilst waiting for my dinner to be served in the smart northern hotel, when the waitress came over and lit a small candle in a glass container in the centre of my table.

She said my meal wouldn't be long in coming, so I continued reading and drinking. Imagine my consternation as I realised my broadsheet newspaper was now well alight, having fallen open over the candle.

Luckily, no one else was in the restaurant so I spilt some of the beer over the flames then cleaned up the mess with several linen napkins that were on my table and others nearby.

I had just finished restoring order when the young lady returned with my meal. Looking rather concerned, she asked what had happened to the napkins. Sheepishly, I explained I'd dropped my beer, and handed her the sodden napkins. In exchange, I received a new supply and a clean cloth was put on the table.

I didn't stay for a sweet or coffee, but, instead, retired to the bar. A brandy helped me be thankful that the overhead sprinkler system had not been activated over the party of elderly diners that had arrived to sit at nearby tables.

At breakfast next morning, I felt a distinct 'chill' from the staff. I'm sure they had studied the remains of my attempt …

**… at setting fire to their place of work.**

## GOLF – A GAME TO DIE FOR?

When visiting a golf and country club located on the rolling slopes of the Blue Ridge Mountains, east of Sydney, Australia, I took lunch in the 'smart and yet laid-back' restaurant.

A contradiction in terms for sure, so too the disarming advertisement printed on the back of the paper napkin at my place-setting, offering the services of the local town's funeral and burial company!

Looking around, I was certainly one of the youngest diners, although not in the first bloom of youth. Outside, the players, too, had seen better days. In many cases, quite some years ago.

**It seemed the funeral arranging organisation had certainly done their research on prospective customers!**

## HE AIN'T HEAVY, HE'S MY FRIEND

I was making enquiries in a hospital, along with my African colleague. When I asked the way to an office, staff mischievously guided me through the mortuary. We fell over dead bodies and my colleague fainted. He was of a small stature so I picked him up, put him over my shoulder and found the way out. On reaching daylight a local yelled, 'Stop thief!'

**Is this what they mean by the 'voodoo man'?**

## I BOUGHT AN ORIGINAL FLYING CARPET

If you go to the Blue Mosque in the centre of Istanbul, a most wonderful building decorated in blue Arabic-design tiles, look out for the area's 'tourist hunters'.

These are young Turkish people, who speak good English and several other languages, and who work on a commission basis to catch the unwary traveller and invite them to their 'uncle's' nearby carpet shop.

Having time before a sunny afternoon flight home, I was easily snared by such a skilled operator. *However, what he didn't know was that I actually wanted to buy a Turkish carpet.* Therefore, as the pickup started, I was actually a willing candidate for his questions:

Was I from London?

Once he knew I was a Londoner, which football team did I support, Arsenal or Spurs?

What did I think of David Beckham?

Did I live near the Queen of England?

Smiling at his efforts to engage me, I followed his footsteps into the nearby souk, a mixture of winding lanes, tight pavements and small shops near to the famous underground Roman Cistern. Upon entering the carpet store of his supposed uncle, I was invited to sit on a very low sofa and take Turkish tea with him and the owner, who welcomed me to his emporium.

Explanations followed for all the different types of carpet that were stylishly displayed, both in groups on the floor and as wall hangings. The owner skilfully led me to explain that I was interested in purchasing a small one for the entrance hall of my house in England. As he began to throw a range of large carpets in front of me, I quickly explained that my house was not that big. I could see his disappointment.

I was relaxed with his sales technique as my flight was not until early afternoon. However, time soon slipped by, as tea continued to be poured, different carpets displayed and many questions asked. This was all aimed at getting me to focus on a particular size and type of carpet and move me to a purchasing decision.

*The second thing the owner and his assistant didn't know was that my business friends in the organisation I'd been visiting during the week had told me how to haggle and position my price questions. I'd also been advised to ensure that I carried a range of currencies – in cash – to avoid the trap of paying excessive credit card charges.*

'Uncle's' patience began to wane as I still hadn't made a choice, or agreed a price, and I was beginning to realise I must do so or things would get unpleasant. Luckily, it was just then that the driver of the taxi, which 'Uncle' had earlier kindly arranged to take me to the airport, came into the store and a decision was demanded. I had actually seen the carpet I liked some time earlier and it was still on display. Now it was only a question of price in the currency that gave the best value to me rather than the shop owner. 'Uncle' started asking about the credit card. I said no thanks. Next, he asked if I had dollars I said yes, his eyes lit up thinking of the enhanced exchange rate he would get. I said I needed them at the airport and a scowl followed.

Lastly, I offered Turkish lira. I swear I could have heard a pin drop for, at this time, the country's currency had not been devalued and so I was carrying many 1,000,000 lira notes in my wallet. (To give some idea of their value, one US dollar was worth approximately 1,500,000 Turkish lira; a very advantageous exchange rate. It would, therefore, be an extremely good value purchase – to me – but a very poor sale to him!)

Before he could refuse my offer, I peeled off the required number of notes from my 'wad', handed them over and all of us watched, in silence, as my bargain was wrapped in brown paper and tied with string.

*As my carpet and I flew out of the store, and into the taxi, I could see, and hear, that 'Uncle' was berating his relative for trapping such a mean and worthless shopper that morning.*

## I'D HEARD OF MONEY LAUNDERING BUT THIS WAS REAL CLEANING

I was working for several weeks in a distant, small Asian country and went to the (central) bank in the capital city to change a $100 bill. It was refused because the note had a small tear that had been repaired with Sellotape. However, it was a genuine bill with identical serial numbers at both ends of the note.

So I asked for the manager.

He was a floor manager, or something like that, and he also refused the note, so I asked for his boss – who also refused the note. They explained that they would only change clean, unspoilt bills. Sensing my frustration, he suggested that I saw a Director and very soon, I ended up talking to the Governor of the country's central bank!

In a polite conversation, I suggested that they probably had many nice clean $100 bills in their vaults. 'Oh yes, of course, all neatly wrapped in bundles of 100' came the proud reply.

The Golf Lynx

'Well,' I said, 'why don't you take my $100 note and exchange it with one of those from the middle of a bundle – no one will ever know.' 'What an excellent idea,' came the reply.

He took my note and a few minutes later came back with a nice clean one – and proceeded to change it himself into the local currency. Problem solved! How's that for customer care?

**Could we expect that same level of service from the Governor of the Bank of England located in Threadneedle Street, London?**

## I THINK THIS WAS MEANT TO BE

We had no real evidence to support the idea that we were related to an ancient family from France, but there was a generally accepted view that we were. The idea had been passed down to my father from a distant uncle, who had apparently had some research done, over 30 years ago, into the family history.

All that we knew about the possible ancestors at this point was that they had come over to England with William the Conqueror in 1066 and had occupied Dunster Castle in North Somerset. There was perhaps the hint that the original De Mohun had come from a place called Mohun, or perhaps Moyon, close to the town of St Lo, Normandy.

My father's rather vague statement 'that there was a possible connection between our name and the De Mohuns' had lodged in the back of my mind but quickly passing years had ensured, until now, that I had neither time nor inclination to pursue my ancestry.

However, having just changed my career, a family holiday motoring through France to the Pyrenees was chosen as a celebration, especially as we could, after travelling over on the ferry from Weymouth to Cherbourg, spend a day in St Lo and see if we could find out anything about the De Mohuns.

(I have to say at this point that none of the rest of my family, apart perhaps from my mother, who loved history, had any interest whatsoever in pursuing this vague family connection. 'While you are there you had better check out the family chateau,' she suggested, half-jokingly and, I suspect, a little hopeful that the – supposed – De Mohun connection might uncover some wealthy French relatives.)

After a calm channel crossing, we drove to the town hall of St Lo where I got the typical Gallic shrug in answer to my enquiries about any Mohun family records.

I learned that, during the invasion in 1944, the Germans and the Allied Forces had, between them, pretty well flattened St Lo, and that all the town's historical records were lost. It seemed that nothing remained, and looking at some of the photographs of the wartime damage, it was easy to believe.

The following day, we decided to forget the ancestors and move on South to our next destination, Rennes in Brittany. Whether by accident or, as I now believe, by someone else's design, soon after setting off we got lost while getting out of St Lo and found ourselves on a minor country road leading we knew not where.

We nearly turned back but it was a lovely morning, the countryside was very pretty and I knew we were driving in roughly the right direction, so we decided to press on when suddenly, a couple of kilometres later, my wife shouted and pointed to a wooden finger post. 'It says Moyon, isn't that what you are looking for?'

'Well I'm not sure,' I said. 'But we had better go and see what's there.' My heart skipped a beat as we soon found ourselves driving down a narrow lane towards a tiny rural hamlet with a large stone farmhouse with outbuildings, a duck pond and a very small chapel.

I made the assumption, which later proved to be erroneous, that we had arrived at the village of Moyon. We parked the cars and I got out, walked to the farmhouse door and knocked. After what seemed a long wait, a youngish woman appeared, looking slightly nervous, with a cluster of children ranging in age from about two to ten peering at me from behind her skirt.

'Bonjour Madame, je m'appelle Moon ou Mohun ou Moyon.'

I bumbled on in Franglais trying to explain that we were looking for information about my possible ancestors. She smiled but looked rather nonplussed then said, disarmingly, 'Je ne comprends pas Monsieur. Un moment.' She called back into the house and her husband appeared – dark, good looking, dressed in dungarees, every inch a French farmer. I repeated my little story emphasising Mohun and Moyon, lineage, even 1066 then throwing in hopefully, 'Le Chateau?'

Suddenly, his face lit up with comprehension. He spoke rapidly with his wife and the children and everyone seemed very excited. They rushed out of the door talking and gesticulating. The farmer went into the yard at the side of the house and roared out again in a dilapidated 'deux chevaux' car!

The rest of his family piled in except for a couple of the older ones who jumped on bicycles. He motioned for me to get back in my Jaguar.

'Suivez, suivez,' he shouted, and set off down the lane.

We travelled in convoy. Within a few hundred metres, the 'deux chevaux', followed by our convoy, swung off the road into a grassy field. We bumped through a rutted gateway, where I feared for my car springs, and across a second field arriving in a cloud of dust in front of a substantial earthwork surrounded by rose bay willow herb and an insignificant wire fence.

I noticed a rather dilapidated notice board hanging off one of the fence posts as we climbed out of the car and the farmer proudly pointing to the area in front of us 'C'était le Chateau Moyon,' he shouted.

My mother's flippant remark had turned into an amazing reality. We were standing at the entrance to somewhere that had perhaps been the home of my ancestors very, very many years before. For, on close inspection, the notice board revealed that the site was a protected monument and that it was indeed the original home of Guillaume de Moyon.

I was filled with emotion. A wrong road, a chance decision to keep on it and not turn back, calling at the first house we saw, and now being led directly to the ruins of an ancestral home of which we had had no previous knowledge, made me think that somehow this moment had been predestined.

I felt sure, without any of the knowledge and evidence that was to follow, that I was being pulled slowly, but inevitably, towards the past and …

***… I really was descended from the ancient De Mohun family and, now, had to live up to 900 years of history.***

Postscript: Readers might like to read the full story behind this coincidence. Search Amazon Books for 'Moonshadow' by Michael G. Moon.

## LATER WE REALISED WHY THEY WANTED US OUT OF THE WAY

The week-long conference consisted of a series of presentations, timed between 9.00 am and 12 noon, and between 2.00 pm and 4.00 pm each day, and I was one of the team of British experts chosen to explain, using Mandarin text on overhead projector slides and printed hand-outs, various Western management and business development techniques to over 100 senior and important Chinese government officials. Impressively, they were seated ten to a row, in ten rows, filling part of the large hall of the Local University.

After Monday morning's opening address and welcome, a colleague presented the first of several technical topics. His session took us comfortably to noon, the time for lunch, at which point we were promptly taken from our seats of honour, on the stage, and led to a guest suite upstairs.

Here, a member of the organisation's support staff showed us the complex of rooms put at our disposal for the whole week, particularly opening the doors to single bedrooms of the sort I'd last seen at university. The kitchen and dining area was also highlighted, so, too, the buffet of Chinese delicacies awaiting us.

Before this official left us, we made sure we gave our thanks for such hospitality, stressing it was more than we had expected and asking, 'Could we not eat with the delegates?' With much embarrassment, we were told that as guests and senior speakers we must sleep, to refresh ourselves, before returning to the hall and commencing our afternoon talks.

On our own, we shared our surprise and amusement and, whilst enjoying our lunch, spent the time checking our slides and documents. At 1.55 pm, we were collected and taken back to the hall where, to applause, we were invited to resume our places on the stage.

The ritual of being taken upstairs at noon and collected for the 2.00 pm start was repeated on Tuesday and Wednesday. By this time, rather than bemused, we were becoming cross that our valuable teaching time was being wasted by an unnecessary extra-long midday break.

During Thursday's lunch, I had occasion to leave our suite to seek the conference host. Getting lost, and using the wrong staircase to descend, I pushed open the door, which I thought was our return entrance, only to realise it was just a side door looking straight onto all of the delegates still at lunch. However, they were not eating, as this was at least 90 minutes into the two-hour break. Rather, they were, with some animation and cheering, watching a Chinese Kung Fu film!

Fortunately, they did not observe me observing them, so I was able to return to my colleagues and explain what I'd seen. So as not to cause political embarrassment between our respective groups, we decided to keep this knowledge to ourselves, especially as only Friday remained for the ritual.

During that day's lunchtime, and having looked through the side door to observe the audience watching another film, we agreed that the organiser had really provided our upstairs venue and extra hospitality for the delegates' benefit rather than ours …

**... fitting the films into each day's schedule by keeping us upstairs 'asleep'!**

## LIFE REALLY IS STRANGER THAN FICTION

*Alan Titchmarsh, gardener, writer and broadcaster of very many radio and television programmes has kindly provided this reminiscence of the time he was with colleagues, filming Ground Force, a BBC television show, in which he and fellow presenters, Charlie Dimmock and Tommy Walsh, would perform a makeover on a garden. It was whilst filming one of these events that Alan remembers the following conversation – which certainly supports the heading of this chapter.*

Willie, our Irish builder on 'Ground Force', was chatting to me one day at the end of a shoot. Out of the corner of his eye, he saw a lorry load of turf being transported down the road.

'That's what I'm going to do when I get a lot of money,' he remarked.

'What?' I asked.

'Send me lawn away to be cut.'

## WELCOME TO CHINA, NEW FRIENDS, A CLEVER TAXI SCAM, SOME DANGER, MUCH STRESS

A chauffeur in a large black limousine, sent from the office of the mayor of Tianjin, usually met me at the original Beijing Airport. This was both a courtesy to a Westerner, working on behalf of the Chinese Government and the World Bank, and a way of avoiding paying the exorbitant fees charged by the private enterprise taxis that illegally touted for business at the terminal door.

On this occasion, arriving at 2.00 pm on a Sunday afternoon, tired after leaving my London home at 6.00 am the previous day, I found to my surprise that there was no official car to greet me or my two briefcases and two suitcases (I was going to stay for quite some time).

In the days before mobiles with international roaming, the only way to make contact with my office was by landline from the special desk inside the terminal. I say 'special' as you joined a long queue in front of two stern-looking female telephonists sitting behind armoured glass. When you reached one of them, you handed in, through the gap at the bottom of the glass, a small form on which you had written the phone number you required them to dial. My operator, no name on display, demanded to see my cash having calculated how much a five-minute local call would cost. It seemed they expected callers to have enough money to make 'good conversation'.

Satisfied with my credit worthiness, she dialled the local office in Tianjin, the city I was going to work in, then slipped the handset, attached to a short length of telephone cord, under the glass screen so that I could – bending down – use it to ask, strongly, 'Where's the car?' The office colleague's voice registered much surprise and consternation that I was still at the airport and not sitting in the comfort of the limousine and being driven towards my hotel. This person didn't know what to do as they were sure there was only the one limousine available that day, so we both hung up in frustration.

Next, I showed the operator the telephone number of my colleagues in the project team, based at the company's offices in England. Once more, she pointed to the money I held and then confirmed I had enough to pay for this call. 'Any changes to the usual limo arrangements?' I asked over the faint connection. Again, no one knew why the car wasn't waiting for me, so I said goodbye and handed the phone back. No refund was given, so I assumed the costs were accurate – but I had no way of knowing.

It was at this point, between about 3.00 pm and 4.00 pm, that a smartly dressed Chinese businessman, or that's what I thought he was, approached me and said, in good English, 'I have been watching you since your plane arrived and you seem to be having difficulties.' I felt I had found a new friend.

Turning round, he beckoned to several Chinese men standing by an outer door of the terminal outside of which was parked a very smart silver Mercedes saloon car. He explained that this was his personal car, one of the men was his chauffeur and, as a gesture of goodwill and with proper payment, they would both be put at my disposal and take me to my destination. He seemed especially pleased when I explained it was at least a three to four-hour drive away, showing him the Chinese name of the hotel I was to stay in.

Some discussion between us, but mainly on his side, encouraged me to agree a payment of 900 yuan. (A discount on the 1,000 yuan he had first requested.) As China was now 'reopening' after the Tiananmen Square tensions in Beijing, I knew either sum to be a large cash payment. However, I was past caring, seeking only to travel quickly to get a shower and a beer at my hotel.

Unfortunately, before I could travel in his car, I needed more Chinese money to pay him the full amount 'up-front'. He kindly told me all I had to do was go upstairs to the currency exchange office on the mezzanine floor. I did, with my luggage, and found the exchange was a room at the end of a long corridor with a small counter hatch built into its door, a clerk behind it and a very large, almost walk-in, safe with its door open behind him. That meant I could draw cash against some of the travellers cheques I was carrying.

Yes, I certainly could cash them, but only after completing several documents in triplicate and having my passport studied and copied to make sure I was a bona fide visitor and not a currency fraudster!

As I returned to the waiting businessman, I realised I seemed to be the last European in the terminal building and he had gathered extra 'drivers', all keen to see me pay for my trip. Little did I know that this was only the first instalment of several payments I would be expected to make once we had set off.

Sitting in the back of the Mercedes felt good, but lonely, as unlike in a London cab, the driver did not want to discuss the government of the day, or ask about Manchester United or any other British football clubs. After the earlier stress, I was actually pleased the journey was silent as we joined the ring road, leading to the motorway going south to Tianjin.

I almost dozed off, but 'wait a minute', we're stopping on the hard shoulder at the entrance to the motorway. Without a moment's delay, the driver began unloading my luggage from the boot and I started asking, 'What on earth is happening?' Without answering, all he could do was show me that I should get into a very small, bright yellow, diesel 'pop-pop' taxi-truck that had suddenly pulled up behind us.

It was obvious I could not argue, I did not know where we were and my luggage was already loaded. As I climbed into the rear of this new vehicle, I noticed it had a metal grille between my area and the two front seats, and the Mercedes had done a neat turn around and was speeding back the way we had come. I was trapped.

My new driver was also silent and, it seemed, intent on killing both of us as he proceeded to drive, and stay, in the middle lane, ignoring all other traffic that sped past on either side. This was especially disconcerting when huge, diesel Chinese Army people-carriers drove up close behind us then, on overtaking, all the soldiers gesticulated in a variety of international hand signals (you know what I mean) at me and the taxi.

This experience lasted for about an hour when, at an intersection, we stopped again on the hard shoulder. From out of the trees came a new Chinese person who proceeded to climb into the cab's spare front seat. Foolishly, but in my frustration, I asked the driver who was this? 'Friend, friend,' was the quick reply. He and the driver then proceeded to talk, in Mandarin, as we drove on for about another hour, completely ignoring me sitting in the back, as well as more of those army lorries trying to overtake us.

By this time, it was getting dark and I could see the lights of a motorway toll station ahead. More alarmingly, I could also see a soldier in uniform standing in the lane we were using and holding a large machine gun, which was definitely pointed at our vehicle as we slowed towards the barriers.

On stopping, the soldier pointed and shouted that we must all get out and stand against the taxi. Traffic, of course, was still going either side of us. He then made it clear that I must stand absolutely still – which I was certainly doing – as he marched the driver and his front seat passenger across the carriageway to the tollbooth office.

Marching them back after about ten minutes, the friend surprisingly said in good English. 'We can go now,' and we did. However, as soon as we were through the barrier, he turned to me and said 'You owe the driver 100 yuan as he's had to pay a fine on your behalf!' Apparently, one of the Army trucks had reported us for being a safety obstruction and this is why we were arrested when we got to the tollbooths.

I asked, 'Why should I be blamed and pay the fine?' He said I was the reason they were on the motorway. (Privately, I admitted there was logic in the answer, but that the style of driving was certainly not of my choosing.)

The friend then said that if I didn't pay they would stop and throw me out – wherever we were. As luck would have it, I had a 100 yuan note left from my expenses in the airport but, before handing it over, I stressed, with some force in my voice, 'I have already paid 900 yuan for this trip. Why should I pay more?'

The driver, when he heard this information translated to him into Mandarin, started screaming, using, I assumed, appropriate swear words. His friend then turned to me and explained that the businessman in the airport, who had set all this up, was only paying this driver 100 yuan for the whole journey. Therefore, if I didn't pay the toll, he would have done the whole thing for free.

I began to feel sympathy for the driver, anger at the businessman and foolish for having entered into the arrangement in the first place. But, as I was now definitely trapped, I handed over my last note.

Shortly after this activity, we approached the outskirts of the city and began to leave the motorway at its first major intersection. Whereupon, the taxi truck stopped, the driver's friend got out and, before leaving, turned and said how much he had enjoyed meeting me. I felt there was no polite answer to that given he had had a free ride on my account.

It was now 8.00 pm and, as the occasional overhead streetlight illuminated our journey, I had begun to recognise some landmarks I'd seen on a previous visit.

Turning into what I knew was the 'Western Quarter', we arrived at the entrance of a hotel I certainly recognised. It was the one we had used before, but it was not the one I should now be staying in!

We stopped at the main doors and the concierge began to approach our vehicle. Before he could remove my luggage, I was out and dragging the driver by the arm into the foyer. Thank goodness, I thought, I recognize the same front-of-house reception and security staff from previous visits.

The driver, of course, was not taking my action quietly, so people were beginning to notice the commotion we were making, but I made it to the check-in desk and smiled at the duty manager, who also recognised me. I briefly explained the struggle it had taken to get from Beijing and that we were now in the wrong place. As I spoke, I showed her the confirmation letter of my new booking and apologised for not staying in her hotel.

She began to give the driver directions to the new location. Whereupon he, with much shouting, told her he needed more money to drive, apparently another 30 minutes further into the centre of the city. She explained this to me. I reminded her I was here on government business, had been tricked at the airport, had now spent 1,000 yuan and – 'enough was enough'. I then asked her to call for the police!

Other reception desk staff and nearby Chinese guests were shocked by this demand. Not an action to be taken lightly in their country. When this request was relayed to the driver he collapsed in front of me, obviously pleading 'don't do it.'

My tiredness and compassion fought each other but, through the receptionist, I obtained a promise that he would drive me the rest of the way using the directions and map that she was kindly giving him.

We returned to his taxi and set off towards this new part of the city. Several stops to ask the way, not by me but the driver using his lighter to illuminate the map to passers-by, got us to a residential area where there were certainly no smart hotels. Instead, down a cul-de-sac where, on stopping at the end, I thought I was about to 'meet my maker'.

I say that as the driver's behaviour and language was now extremely threatening but – it transpired – was directed towards himself for getting lost, not at me for the experiences of the journey.

After almost an hour (not the promised 30 minutes), we arrived at the correct location both breathing a large 'sigh of relief'. Just as we stopped by the front door, several of my colleagues, who were walking into the hotel having finished a good dinner at the adjacent restaurant, came over and enquired, 'Where have you been?'

Needless to say, I ignored such a fatuous question and instead, asked one of them for some change and gave it to the driver. He was extremely pleased. As I entered the foyer, I calculated, from the hotel clock, that it was about 40 hours since I had left home, was lucky to have arrived and …

*… I really did need a cold shower and a beer in order to calm down!*

Postscript: Next day in the office I learnt a variety of information, which I now share:

1) The limo had broken down on the way to the airport and, because I had exited through the wrong gate of the terminal, I had missed the minibus with a relief driver that had been sent to collect me.

2) Most alarmingly, if I had taken note of any sort of registration number of the Mercedes, or the taxi-truck, they'd have been looked for by the national police force and 'dealt with'.

3) I dreaded to think what that meant as the Mayor's office said that, if caught, the perpetrators would be punished very severely as he, and an important guest to their country, had been insulted by this scam.

*In a way, I was glad I did not have that information for, whilst still smarting over the switch-over trick to which I had been subjected, I grudgingly admired, from the safety of the office, the entrepreneurial spirit of the taxi team involved. It was as good as any I had seen in London.*

## POSTSCRIPT

*'Dear reader, if you have enjoyed reading the stories in this book whilst on holiday then I am sorry that I might be alarming you as you read the following entry. You could be realising something worryingly embarrassing as you get towards the end of the story.*

*However, if you haven't yet gone on holiday, then I urge you to remember the following anecdotes in order that you don't repeat the stupidity of the author of the recollections and this book.'*

## DAMN THIS TECHNOLOGY – THERE'S NO FUN ANYMORE

I can recall it was at least three times, in a very busy year, when, arriving back late at night at one of the many different car parks located around the perimeter of Heathrow airport – tired after long flights, days away, and many business meetings – that I found my car had gone missing from where I thought I'd left it!

*Until fairly recently, I would have been surprised if that had not happened to you\*.*

Anyway, on those occasions, each separated by some months, I got to know the parking attendants well. They drove me around the extensive lots in their service van until I found my car – exactly where I had left it – but certainly not where I had been looking.

### To quote my hero, Homer Simpson – 'Doh!'

\*I can suggest this as you have probably already downloaded onto your iPhone: 'My Car Locator Free'. It is the easiest to use free car locator in the Google Play Store, with all the essential information displayed at all times. This app uses your GPS to remember where you park with the push of just one button and guides you back to your car easily. Never again forget where you have parked! It's also great for remembering the location of your hotel, camping spot, boat jetty, bus stop or any other location you would like to easily return to later.

Also, if you accept the quotation (attributed to the American author, Ralph Waldo Emerson) that 'Life is a journey, not a destination,' then your location pinpointed absolutely through the wonder of the World Wide Web may, I suggest, take the fun (?) out of walking around airport car parks, tired and late at night.

On the other hand, it can still be an interesting experience to arrive back in such car parks, as I did twice, only to realise that I had left my car keys on the desk of the office I was working in elsewhere in Europe. Forgetting them as I rushed to get away to grab a taxi to the airport, in order to return home on the last flight of the day.

Fortunately, I had a car insurance policy that provided a free breakdown rescue service. However, I don't think it was intended to be used on these occasions. Anyway, I took advantage of the kind offer to transport me and my locked car home. Of course, this was in the early hours of the morning, so I was certainly not popular with my wife, nor the neighbours, as the transporter craned my car onto the driveway of my house.

It didn't help when the same driver transported me home the second time for, as he lowered my car onto the drive, one of the four support legs of the transporter punctured the pavement in front of our house. The local city council were not amused when they had to do an emergency repair to fill the large hole that had – mysteriously, or so I told them – appeared.

As you're sitting there on holiday, just remind yourself where you parked your car. If you can't remember, you might soon be having as much fun as I have had. On the other hand, if you're about to go on holiday, then please ensure you have the My Car Locator Free app (or another) loaded on your phone, and make sure you take your keys with you!

Lastly, please remember the prophetic words of Lin Yutang, a Chinese writer, translator, linguist and inventor, who lived between 1895 and 1976:

**'No one realises how beautiful it is to travel until he comes home and rests his head on his old, familiar pillow.'**

I hope you will agree. Thanks for reading my book.

**Bon Voyage**                                                                  **Andrew**

## ABOUT THE AUTHOR AND STORY COLLECTOR

Andrew P. Wiltshire has spent 30 years working and travelling in 40 countries, successfully leading the completion of over 60 management consultancy projects. In addition, he has fulfilled senior executive roles in British manufacturing organisations and been a Visiting Fellow with lecturing responsibilities at four international universities. He lives with his wife, Moira, and two Border terrier dogs in Essex, England.

He draws on his business and personal experiences, together with those of a wide selection of friends and business contacts, to create this collection of true travel and life stories in the Humorous Hassle book. In telling them, he has two ambitions. To:

• Make all readers laugh and smile.

• Donate the profits from every sale to the Salvation Army Homelessness Services Charity.

Now, please visit this book's website **www.tap.uk.com** for more information about a talk that features some of the anecdotes from this book **that will make listeners laugh and smile**, as well as other presentations that Andrew is delighted to give*.

These events, like this book, are **to raise money for charity**. Rotary clubs, WIs, U3A and other social meeting groups, local history societies, retirement fellowships and guests at after dinner engagements have already enjoyed them. Any group you belong to can, too.

*These are entitled: Where is the Fog?, The Last Hussar of the 20th, and Who was Beatrix Potter's Secret Code Breaker?*

## ACKNOWLEDGEMENTS

I have not named the originator after each tale. Instead, I have placed their initials, shown below, after their story's title in the index. Each person can, if they wish, highlight their item/s to family members or friends, some of whom may not have heard these tales before. So, 'Thank you.'

Peter Allen (PA) Piet van Amelrooij (PvA) Nigel Bagley (NAB), Martin Beckwith-Brown (MBB), John Bowler (JFB), Jackie Breeze (JB), Mike Breeze (MB), Nicholas Comfort (NC), Ian Crawford (IC), Sami Dakhalia (SFD), Victoria Derry-Thomas (VDT), Ryan Edwards (RJE), Adrian Foale (AJF), Gary Gerds (GG), Russell Greenwood (RG), Godfrey Hall (GH), Robin Halls (RVH), Robin Hemmings (RAH),

Ken Hornett (KGH), Ian Hudson (IBH), Jenny King (JK), Michael Moon (MGM), Roger Neville (RDN), Christine Ottaway (CIO), Adam Pierzchala (AP), Susanne Pinnock (SP), Matthew Radford (MR), Dave Robinson (DR), Terry Russell (TJR), Gale Salmon (GS), John Saunders (JS), Margaret Spoors (MS), David Tennet MBE (DST), Jeremy West (JW), Stuart White (SEW), Russell Wiltshire (REW) and Richard Yallop (JRY).

Additionally, I particularly wish to mention John Barnard (JB) who, although he says I volunteered, sent me to China. He is, therefore, one of the reasons I can recall the fog story that is the book's lead story, as well as several other experiences I enjoyed in what is now the last century. These events really are ancient history given how that country has changed since then. Dave Barker (DEB) is another 'old China hand' who provided similar stories.

Receiving an entry from Jack Straw (JWS), before his retirement as an MP, was a pleasure, adding as it does further gravitas to our fund raising efforts. The help of Dan Sleat in enabling me to include this story is especially appreciated. So, too, Tim Marsh's (TM), like Jack and I, another contributor and former young scout in a troop on the outskirts of Epping Forest. When you read about Jack's 'Political Clean Sweep' flight, you may be glad that you never have to visit the airfield that he mentions.

The assistance of Mark Simonsson, in gaining the permission of Rory Bremner (RKOB) to retell the time I met him on a train going north from London, is also valued.

The anecdote from Alan Titchmarsh (AT), after another meeting, provides a wry observation on how his television show colleague felt his life could be made better. Perhaps many of us, who have to mow the lawn in our gardens, have the same ambitions as his co-worker.

Having the help of Chris Shipley of Downs & Co, Alison Pearson (AP) and Dawn O'Driscoll of the Daily Telegraph and Vivienne Clore of the Richard Stone Partnership, in confirming permission to use published material and stories, is also gratefully acknowledged.

So, too, is the encouragement and support of Robert Lee and Major Martin Hill of the Salvation Army.

The formatting and proofing of the book's stories, whatever size and content, would not have been possible without the care, enthusiasm and professionalism of Mary Sandall (MS), Joanne Moore (Hodges), James Ellison and especially Melodie Pike. They have each coped with the challenge of improving my writing style for your benefit.

They have also given me invaluable help and suggestions whilst we have produced this book.

However, the editorial opinions expressed are my own and any inaccuracies are my responsibility and not theirs, or the printers Blackwell Print.

Whilst writing about my own experiences and collecting and editing the stories from the contributors, I have enjoyed the critical feedback and encouragement of Moira, my wife. Superbly, she has fulfilled her role as my 'Base Camp Manager' and, with the support of our children, Charlotte and Russell, has enabled me to roam the world enjoying challenging consultancy assignments, flight delays, dodgy hotels and dubious meals, secure in the knowledge that, on my safe return, they would anticipate – with pride – the telling of the fun (?) I had had.

Lastly, I must thank a wide group of unknown authors and sign writers who have created the various newspaper headings, comments and public notices given at the start of each chapter. I have read, noted and enjoyed these items in cities across six continents of the world and over my 40 years of travelling.

With my ambition to make readers smile, I could not resist reprinting some of them here. I hope you will agree that these, the stories and the cartoons embody the important thought that in these challenging times …

**… *laughter is still the best medicine for coping with them!***

## INDEX

## POSTSCRIPT